CW01481005

QUENCHING

Collective Security and Nonviolence

Howard Horsburgh

Pax Books

i

Published in 1992 and distributed by
Pax Books
c/o George Paxton
87 Barrington Drive
Glasgow G4 9ES

•

ISBN :   0 9519022 0 2

Printed by
Clydeside Press
37 High Street
Glasgow G1 1LX

Love is nothing but quenched wrath

The Cloud of Unknowing

To Hengist and Cordelia

TABLE OF CONTENTS

Preface.

Page

1. Animals Seeking Security.   1

2. Humans Seeking Security.   7

3. Multilateralism, Unilateralism, and Gorbachev.   24

4. Pacifying the Planet.   31

5. The Moral Weapon.   40

6. The Problems of Non-violence.   68

7. Conflict and Intervention.   87

PREFACE

This is not a book of expertise let alone the fruit of research (in any legitimate sense of that much abused word). I hope it sometimes deals in facts. But the facts it deals in are only the grosser ones that should be familiar to us all, not the rarefied findings of experts. This is because it is grounded in the belief that security — like many other things — stands in greater need of less conventional and more comprehensive reflection than of additional floods of arcane information.

If we escape the nemesis of being too clever by half we won't owe it to experts but to an enhanced overall grasp of the problems of security. This depends on openness to novelty, and on width and many-sidedness of view, more than on detailed knowledge; and it is to these neglected but pressing needs that I aspire to contribute, partly by reminding us that <u>homo sapiens</u> is the Hairless Ape and partly by insisting that he is more, much more, because he is at least a moral agent and perhaps a Child of God; and that these 'extras' should make all the difference to how he seeks security.

I have allowed myself a few lighter moments, in spite of the seriousness of my subject. I've been thinking about it since my pre-war teens; and after so many years of desperate seriousness lighter moments are the only substitute for pills — and I have to take enough of them already.

Chapter 1

ANIMALS SEEKING SECURITY

Till Darwin took a different view Mother Nature was thought of as an amazingly ingenious as well as versatile woman. Surviving has always been her principal business, and think how cunningly and variously her children have sought it!

Let's begin by considering the main devices that animals have used in this quest.

To begin with, security is often sought through flight; and, in some species, flight is the most important means of ensuring survival. For example, antelopes, are always running away, and they can do it so quickly that it takes a cheetah to catch one. Flight is also one of the common human ways of safeguarding ourselves. Other animals have tried to secure it through some kind of inaccessibility. Hedgehogs, armadilloes and the creatures which play dead illustrate three sorts of inaccessibility. Their methods haven't been lost on humans, who, over the centuries, have sought inaccessibility in many ways: through taking to the mountains, jungles and deserts, or through starting a new life on a remote island; through building castles, moats, mazes and catacombs; and by playing dead. Still other animals have sought security by developing some form of protective colouring that is supposed to hide them wherever they are. For example the zebra of the African savannas merges into his environment and is hard for the predator to identify. Humans have also adopted this device, wearing dark clothes at night and camouflaging either their possessions or themselves from an enemy. Animals also attack other animals and defend themselves from them. I shall use the term 'defence' for the use of weapons and physical violence as means of survival and dominance. The predator is the ideal illustration of this device since he belongs to a species which has specialised in deadly weapons. Most animals can inflict some damage on other animals if they are cornered, but it is mainly predators which have acquired specially lethal tools with which to kill. Could there be a much more ruthless and efficient instrument for jungle killing than the tiger? Or, in a different setting, the crocodile? Both introduce high standards into the business of killing. But Man is the prince of slaughterers: only an also-ran as a wielder of natural weapons, his brain soon furnished him with an abundance of unnatural weapons. Homo sapiens is not the only creature which uses tools; even birds exploit gravity to crack nuts. But he may be the only tool-user who uses tools to kill with, e.g., the branch of a tree, a dagger. Other predators e.g., animals which form packs, though only modestly endowed with natural weaponry, make up for their individual limitations by combining their strengths and skills. For example, wild dogs combine to hunt their prey, sometimes cooperating in the pursuit of individual animals. Humans have also hunted and fought in packs for millenia, forming bands, tribes, nations, gangs and armies, and coordinating attacks on a common enemy.

Animals have also sought security through submission. As far as I know, this device is not used between species. But intraspecific submission occurs in some social species. For example, wolves have been known to save their lives by exposing their throats to an enemy and trusting to its mercy. Similarly, humans, as a last resort, have often begged for their lives. They have bowed and curtsied, turning co-towing into minor art forms. Kings have also submitted to one another, establishing monarchical pecking orders. A multitude of ordinary men and women have had to learn the etiquettes that are needed to survive in the vicinity of the powerful. Knowing the right forms and addresses has often made all the difference to an individual's fate.

Humans are almost unanimous in their dislike of submission. It is always seen as degrading, and it is often said that honourable humans should die sooner than resort to it. But - as has already been implied - we make a distinction between allowing oneself to be dominated in some degree, and being reduced to begging for mercy, the extreme of submission among humans. The former is seen as sensible and involves no loss of dignity or honour. Even Napoleon had to take orders to begin with. But outright submission - never! Many would sooner die first. And the refusal to fight has always been widely - almost universally - seen as a sign of submission, as a placing of oneself at the feet of one's enemy.

But refusing to fight has also served very different ends. For example, soldiers have refused to fight other soldiers with a view to dishonouring them, to claiming that they are not worthy to be fought with. Also, - and far more importantly - it has been used by Gandhi to usher in a new, and more scrupulous, form of combat.

So far I've been talking about the individual's efforts to ensure its own survival. But animals sometimes try to increase the security of other individual animals. They even combine to do this. But they don't conspire to survive as a group, as humans might do. For example, after World War III the last survivors of humanity, perceiving that homo sapiens had become an endangered species, might conspire to keep itself in existence.

In taking flight, and in many other ways, animals contrive to aid the survival of their species at the same time as they safeguard themselves. But they do it unconsciously. In this respect humans are different. For there have been nihilistic humans with such colossal egos that they'd like to take their species with them - a form of insanity from which other animals appear to be free. On the other hand, humans can also conspire to survive as a species, much as we, here and now, conspire to save pandas from extinction. Unfortunately, many humans conspire harder on behalf of pandas than on behalf of <u>homo sapiens</u>.

Individual humans can also combine to safeguard other members of a particular group or other individual animals. As far as I know, the former device is only found among humans, where bands often defend all their own kind as well as the band itself from other bands and their members. Bands of animals don't seem to join together to protect members of their bands. The devil-predator takes the hindmost.

But individual animals do sometimes lessen their own security in order to increase the security of other individual animals. They produce what I shall call security differentials. Such differentials are found naturally, of course. The animal of high stamina has much more chance of survival than a dispirited weakling. But differentials aren't only found, they are also created. For example, a bear will fight to the death in defence of its young - perhaps even of the young of other bears as well? Humans are the same, only more so. They sometimes create colossal differentials, raising one man's security to levels once unimaginable. For example, President Bush went to Colombia in February 1990. If he'd gone on his own his chances of survival would have been close to zero. But he went with armoured helicopters, battleships and 5000 ground troops. As a result even those billionaire drug barons couldn't stop him from attaining an immensely high level of personal security even in their own backyard.

In the animal kingdom these differentials are usually natural, the mere by-products of an animal's fitness, and owe nothing to the efforts of other animals on its behalf. But, as I have already pointed out, there are exceptions.

Producing such differentials has had a large place in human history, millions of men going to war all the more readily for the belief that they were adding to the security of women and children, and body-guards making a living out of keeping other humans alive. I shall be returning to this subject more than once.

Efforts to add to the security of other animals always appear to be efforts on behalf of this or that particular animal. And any animal not included is positively excluded. But this need not have been the case. In other words, - like humans - animals might have set out to democratise the task of adding to others' security.

Individual animals often contend with other individual animals of their own species. They fight for food, for mates, and for dominance. But in few species are agressive courses persisted in till they have brought about an animal's death. Fights to the death do occur. But fights to a comparatively easy victory are commoner. And so the security which an animal seeks is usually partly from animals of its own kind. But it is mainly from animals of other kinds, from members of alien species. Therefore, their security problem is mainly interspecific and only intraspecific in more or less minor degrees. In this respect also humans are different. They have used all the main security-seeking devices of animals to survive attacks from other species. But escalating weaponry soon brought on a time when threats from other species of animals were hardly perceived as part of the security problem: serious threats almost invariably came from other members of their own species. But humans often prey on one another, smoothing the way to vast social evils by making all manner of distinctions among their own kind, e.g., between Germans and Britons, between lambs and wolves, doves and hawks. These distinctions sometimes function usefully. But they are also, almost invariably, devices for flooding the human scene with prejudice and corpses.

Chapter 2

HUMANS SEEKING SECURITY

Homo sapiens's entry on the world scene did much to change the ways in which security was sought. The two greatest changes it introduced are one bad and the other good. There is also a third change, merely heralded at present, which could revolutionise the subject of security. These two greatest changes are escalation and collective security, the one threatening death to all and the other striving for life for all. These three changes are this book's main themes.

Escalation is even embodied in linguistic usage. For example, the term 'defence', which, on any reasonable view, refers only to one way of seeking security, has become the general word for security-seeking. Most countries have Ministries of Defence. But they concern themselves with every imaginable way of gaining extra security. Escalation has brought about this concentration on weaponry. Again, security-seeking has become so preponderantly the business of safeguarding us from one another that we are apt to forget that animals once posed serious threats to security. Man-eating tigers disrupted village life when they appeared, as was still the case when Jim Corbett hunted them down with a high-powered rifle. Yet now, when 'defence' has come to mean security-seeking in general it doesn't mean safeguarding yourself from animals. Today, the animals we meet are usually pets; and humans have more of a problem letting them into their houses than they have in keeping them out.

Escalation is also written into the history of mimicry. For example, the cliches of mock battle have moved in my lifetime from 'bang, bang', to a stuttering whine which is schoolboy for automatic fire, the much improved tool of present-day slaughter. We may soon hear the ' boom' of nuclear explosion coming from boyish throats.

With a view to getting an all-round view of the phenomenon, I shall consider escalation briefly in relation to all the security-seeking methods I have enumerated. In some, escalation is marked: in others it has been of no serious importance.

Humans probably resort to flight about as much as in earlier times. But their get-away devices have escalated from fast legs to space probes, from speeds that made it hard to visit one's neighbours to speeds that put a girdle round the earth in one brief hour.

The tools of accessibility and inaccessibility have also advanced, tho' less conspicuously. For example, banks now have safes with time-locks, which belong to high-tech. inaccessibility. We are getting harder and harder to reach, and we use more and more methods of attaining unreachability. Playing dead still occurs at scenes of carnage. But there has been no escalation. For playing dead is one of the few things which is still done without the use of tools, even makeup.

Camouflage has become a minor art and a minor science. But the protective-colouring method of gaining security has escalated very little - tho' H.G. Wells foresaw a breakthrough in his book, *The Invisible Man*.

Combining in the interests of defence is now so essential to the use of our more sophisticated weaponry that it has become inseparable from defence. For example, battleships, planes, tanks, etc., all have crews. The scale of modern combining has also grown immensely. For example, armies have grown from scores to hundreds, from hundreds to thousands, and from thousands to millions. At one time they consisted of a few men armed and ready for single combat: now, when fully mobilised, they are apt to consist of all the able-bodied who can be spared from other essential tasks. Also, crack military units - such as that which made history at Entebbe - operate with a death-dealing efficiency which would have dumbfounded Caesar.

This brings us to the subject of defence in a more restricted sense, i.e. to the sense in which it means the use of natural or unnatural weapons to hold off or to attack an enemy. Natural weapons escalate little. Humans have developed martial arts based on some of their natural weapons, but tigers have no martial arts based on their claws. And if there are anthopoids which use sticks and stones to kill with, there is still no sign of them developing slings or bows.

The story of human defence has been very different. Humans' natural weaponry is so poor, especially for such a predatory species, that, from the beginning of their history they were strongly prompted to develop unnatural weaponry. They had an urgent need for tools to kill with. Initially, in so far as weapons were developed for use against other species, this inventiveness was checked. For once you have developed the weapons that Jim Corbett used, further escalation only leads to barbarities such as exploding bullets and automatic fire. But Man's security problem is created mainly by other humans; and it is this unique security situation which underlies unlimited and illimitable escalation. Escalation in weaponry demands high intelligence and the use of unnatural weapons; and endless suicidal escalation demands serious competition. The animal kingdom does not offer this competition. But humans have to be in top form to get the better of one another, especially if the enemy has been at as much pains to mobilise its talent as we have. The result is unlimited escalation since the point is never reached when either side can afford to say, 'that'll do'. Arms still more deadly or numerous than those we have, may be needed at any moment. They can never come too soon, too abundantly, or too tailor-made for all murderous occasions. Escalation pits the ruthlessly ingenious against the ruthlessly ingenious, as it did in WW2 when the scientists at the command of the United Nations narrowly won the race to the development of atomic weapons. The playing fields of Eton seemed important once it came to be thought that Waterloo could be won on them. Similarly, now that Armageddom can be won in the laboratory, more and more laboratories are being built everywhere and more and more educational systems, the world over, are coming to be dominated by science. Again, more and more of our scientific work has some kind of 'military angle'. The ancient Chinese have been ridiculed for not taking over the world when they discovered gunpowder: today no one, including the Chinese, would be likely to make that kind of 'mistake'.

What about the method of submission? - the least popular means of seeking security, the device that many would die rather than be reduced to. It has not been subject to escalation, in any serious way - though the surrender of one 'plane to another, as has occasionally taken place in air warfare, presents technical problems that would have puzzled those who first begged for mercy. But though there has not been serious escalation there has been (as it seems to me) vital development. This has been due to the popular demand for universal respect, or the insistence that the humblest and least worthy of humans is entitled to be accorded human dignity and a certain measure of respect. Yes, even from those who are forcing them into submission. For without this sort of minimal mutual concession, humans are reduced to slavery - and slavery is an essentially unfitting state for any human.

This is an enormous advance in human thinking, and it is only very recently, reluctantly and partially that it has been made. It is also of the greatest importance to those who press for the triumph of the third great change in human security-seeking, the emergence of Gandhian methods of non-violence.

Animals do not seem to have the dimmest notions of the ideas of 'respect' and 'dignity': they live in a much more practical world of dog-eat-dog and devil-take-the-hindmost. They kill liberally: they rarely enslave. Enslavement is an exercise in self-aggrandisement that requires one to look ahead in a way that animals never do. Animals are often merciless. But their killing is normally functional, and 'nothing personal', carried out without malice or vengefulness, etc. - the things from which such human atrocities as slavery probably spring.

Human freedom created a need for restraints of a new - and moral - kind. The first of these restraints was surely the slowly-emerging concept of mutual respect. When first introduced it did not apply to everyone: victors did not usually concede it to the defeated unless they had shown exceptional courage; husbands conceded it to wives and sometimes to children, but they did not concede it to the populace at large. Most of us had equals, however lofty our status. Equals were respected; but almost invariably respect was not shown to those at the foot of the status ladder. Gentlemen and ladies had to be respected, of course. But no respect needed to be shown to your coachman, your pet West Indian attendant, or to your work people let alone your slaves. However, those from whom respect was withheld invariably rebelled, demanding human recognition and the rights annexed to the human condition. Some humans would continue to possess more property and power than others. But even those with the most had to show respect to those with the least.

Without lingering on this general subject, two things must be noted: first, that the notions of respect and equality are intertwined; and second, that the concept of respect is essentially ambiguous since it refers to two quite different things. A little more needs to be said about this ambiguity. There is the earned respect that is shown when youths proffer autograph books to tennis or pop stars, or when Mother Theresa is given the Nobel Peace Prize; and there is the unearned respect which is shown when Goering - a murderous gangster - HAS to be legally represented at his trial. Rights are being accorded that Goering has done nothing to earn and everything to forfeit; and which, nevertheless, cannot be forfeited. The earned form of respect is not egalitarian; and hence, is of little interest to us. But the unearned form of respect has already dammed back some human nastiness; and, through having set the yeast of egalitarianism to work, it seems likely to do much more for human wellbeing.

As most humans came to accept this minimal form of human equality they developed new feelings of mutual respect. They tended increasingly to look across at their fellows rather than up or down. This did wonders towards abating pointless confrontation and enmity. It also prepared the way for the innovations we now associate with Gandhi although they are often of great antiquity: the devices of non-violent resistance, all of which include a refusal to fight. It did this by making deadly conflicts more and more intolerable. If you love others, or even respect them, you find it either impossible or immensely difficult to kill them. Mutual respect is naturally protective of human life. Initially, the refusal to fight was equated with mere cowardice, with the absence of that spiritedness that resists to the death. But once mutual respect became widespread a new morally acceptable form of the refusal to fight came to be recognised. It was then generally conceded that the refusal to fight need not be based on either cowardice or the assumption of deep-rooted superiority: it could spring from the complete rejection of homicide. Prior to the coming of mutual respect non-violent methods of security-seeking had been used very successfully by the dominated. This is because the best slave strategy is to be slavish. For that is the strategy which is most likely to bring a relatively comfortable life. But when the egalitarian form of mutual respect appeared it became natural for humans to develop a basically new form of non-violence - a form that combines resistance and courage with the refusal to fight, a form that rejects both homicide and submission, and a form that combines resistance to injustice with an unqualified refusal to accept lethal escalations in disputes which it has proved impossible to avoid. Gandhi never tired of emphasising the difference between these new forms of non-violence and the old ones. He called the old ones 'the non-violence of the weak', and the new ones he called 'the non-violence of the strong'. He even claimed that weak non-violence is so morally objectionable that violence is morally preferable to it. For though slavishness is the best strategy for slaves, it is not the best strategy if you ever want to be free. Freedom has to be won in the heart and mind before it can be won in the real world. The non-violence of the weak is displeasing: the non-violence of the strong requires more courage than violence since it requires the resister to endure in cold blood, not sustained by the heat of battle.

Before concluding this discussion I wish to enter two <u>caveats</u>. First the dawn of respect does not make non-violent methods of confrontation necessary; it only makes them seem honourable and morally tolerable. Killing those we respect is said to be possible. But it is undeniable that as respect flowers into feelings of concern they make non-violent methods ever more essential. Second, Gandhi only systematised 'the non-violence of the strong'; he did not invent it. Methods of non-violent resistance had been used in India from ancient times, and - inspite of what feminists sometimes say, quite perniciously - some women have also practised them from time immemorial. But Gandhi turned scattered practices into <u>satyagraha,</u> a harmless method of resisting any foe, and that is more than enough to make him the man of the century.

The phenomena of escalation taken as a whole - and especially escalation in weaponry - are daunting. Unless humans learn new methods of dealing with conflict another world war will break out and it will be the death of the species. 'People have been saying that since WW1 - and here we still are'. Yes, they have; and the fact that they thought that the end would come sooner does not make it any less true that the end is coming if we disregard the prophets, or that the prophets are wise and far-seeing. Unless we contrive to arrest the process of escalation it will destroy us. That is indisputable; and it is enough in itself to dispose of all present mainstream policies.

2.   Before leaving the topic of violent defence I want to consider some of the things that people urge in its favour.

The main supposed advantage of violent defence in many eyes is that if your armed forces are sufficiently powerful you are BOUND to get your way, regardless of your enemy's qualities or intentions, and he does not need to be trusted or considered in any way whatsoever. Far from depending on his cooperation, it is not even possible for him to stop you getting what you want. But if every war were lost or won, violent defence would still fail as often as it succeeded. But the odds against success are worse than even since some wars are inconclusive and some victories are Pyrrhic. In fact, the claim that we are considering is quite false. In theory, and perhaps one day in practice, a beaten country could turn to the use of non-violent methods of resistance and what arms had failed to win might be won without the use of arms. Such a topsy turvy encounter in which victory emerged from the jaws of defeat would do honour to the spiritual descendants of Spartacus. Again, nobody can be forced to turn into a collaborator. The pressure can mount and mount, and can become hard to resist. But indomitable individuals in all ages have resisted it. We grossly overestimate the power that grows out of the barrel of a gun.

In any case, do we really want our quarrels to go on indefinitely, like the bickering over Alsace and Lorraine? Winning is not enough if it brings no amicable settlement of differences. Or diminution of security problems. And just settlements, those which bring accord, rest on, and give rise to, greater and greater trustfulness.

There is no subject that people show less sense about than trust. Trust is clearly an indispensable part of all social goods; and yet, in film after film, the hero, the chief role model of the entertainment, declares that he trusts NO ONE. As a rule someone is trying to kill him, and one is not surprised.

Pacification settles matters, not victory. As Clemenceau said after World War

I, 'a nation of fifty million does not die'; and while we continue to make war only battles can be won. To win the war we have to abandon the practice of fighting it.

It might also be claimed that whereas, at best, non-violent methods can only be used to defend CAUSES, e.g., ways of life or human rights, violent methods can be used to defend human lives as well. There is some truth in this claim since the heavy-duty defence of people - the kind needed to deal with lethal weapons - DOES involve some degree of violence. But in the eyes of a minority this is actually an advantage since it means that non-violence only defends what we have an indubitable right to defend. But to most of us it sounds like a fatal disadvantage. However, what non-violence cannot defend it can still protect. Let me give the clearest example I know. Adin Ballou in his pioneering book, *Christian Non-resistance*, published 150 years ago, draws attention to it.

In the Irish Troubles of 1798-1800 the Quaker community in Ireland voluntarily disarmed itself. But one Quaker refused to part with his gun. In the fratricidal strife that followed he was the only Quaker casualty. Later on I shall have more to say about this form of security. Among other things I shall claim that when there is point in making comparisons, as in recent revolutions in Eastern Europe, the comparisons tend to show that disputes involving the use of non-violence are less bloody. For example, the Polish revolution was the first and the least costly in terms of human blood. I claim that this was because Walesa used non-violent methods to topple the Communists.

Another advantage that can be claimed for violence is that it enables some people to enjoy a level of security that is much higher than that of the run of people. President Bush's recent visit to Colombia is a good example. If he had gone on his own he would have been unlikely to survive. But he went with land, sea and air forces, and even the drug barons could not get him - not if he did not linger. 'And what, except the threat of violence, could bring him such security?' The answer is 'Nothing!' Non-violent methods can do comparatively little to create security differentials.

Being able to offer higher security to certain people has played a big part in warfare. For example, men have often been willing to go to war because they believed not only that women and children would be safer than themselves but also that the extra risks that they themselves were taking were what brought their loved ones the enhanced security. But such thoughts have dated. Women no longer want or expect more security than men, and thanks to nuclear and other modern weapons children can no longer have more security whether they want it or not. In any case, the advent of political non-violence potentially alters the situation, as I hope to show.

'Well, how do we create such differentials except by violent defence?'

The answer is to be found in two related claims: first, in a substantially non-violent society large security differentials would not be needed; and second, those which would still be desirable could be created adequately through the use of non-violent methods. I shall try to make good these claims in stages.

Many favour violent methods as a last resort because they work to the advantage of wealth. The poorest peasant has all the equipment he needs to engage in non-violent resistance. Non-violence cuts us up or down to the same level, allowing us all to work for juster settlements, But in a world of armaments the race is to the right people - those who can afford the most expensive armaments. (Most people would see the Gulf

War as a good example. Not wanting to concede anything to Gorbachev or the Soviets, others have attributed the demise of the Cold War to the inability of the Soviets to match what the U.S.A. can devote to defence - and more especially to the inability to match 'Star Wars'). Their belief is that wealth is the nearest thing to a sure bet in the life stakes; and they have not gone to all the trouble of collecting it just to forego the advantages it gives them.

In many eyes this advantage outweighs any number of disadvantages. They feel sure that money bags can never be beaten. But they were beaten in Vietnam; and, in the long or moderately long run, wealth is often beaten as it is being beaten in the case of smoking. In the better off parts of the world the cause of smoking is lost and hasn't merely gone out of fashion. But there were formidable tobacco barons long before the new crop of drug barons. We tend to forget that although wealth is hard to beat it is easy to buy provided that you have the money; and the general public does have the money. Business does not forget that people are voters and customers. The rich cannot win against the great tides of events, the long historical drifts. And good causes, the causes of humanity and reason, are winning in their age-long war on callousness, brutality and folly. If the best comes to pass, and homo sapiens reaches his maturity, wealth will lend it support to causes that seem incredibly idealistic at the present time.

In a substantially non-violent world in which wars had ceased, security differentials would be much smaller than they are now. There would be few departures from a more or less high and uniform level of security. Those at greater risk such as leaders and children could be given a larger amount of non-lethal protection. But these extras would only tend to bring them up to normal levels of security. However, that is not objectionable if and when ordinary levels have greatly risen - as they would do in a substantially non-violent society.

The fact is that violence and non-violence can each provide the security differentials which it needs. Colombian levels of security for leaders known to be hostile to the drug barons are probably the lowest on the planet. But defensive methods were able, not merely to cancel those immense risks, but to provide a level of security as high as anyone's. Violence is more than equal to the problems it poses for leaders. But so is non-violence. And it is useless, as some may be tempted to do, to claim that we do not know what a non-violent society would be like. Life, at any given place or time, boils down for all of us to that small tract of country (or sea) that actually surrounds us; and this piece of the world is often reliably non-violent. For example, the hero of a Western is supposed to keep his gun ready to kill with at all times. It takes little to arouse his suspicion and scarcely more to bring him to a quick draw. He bristles through life. But even the near-paranoid are likely to put their guns in a safe place if they wander into a Quaker meeting, an ashram, and perhaps even a knitting circle. They then have a spare hour or two before their next appointment with death. Anyone who lives in an ordinary Western community knows perfectly well what it would be like to live in a non-violent society. It would be simply a more-so version of something they have always known. Safe gatherings have harboured psychopaths, and a gangling knitter who keeps dropping her stitches may soon be showing you that his needle is really a gun. But the odds against such a thing are often immense - and even in a non-violent society your neighbour may go mad and seize the carving knife.

Palme died because he overestimated the level of security that is enjoyed by even a Swedish prime-minister in the absence of special protection. But he was pointing to the sorts of things which the leaders of non-violent countries would enjoy if they cast out that greatest of social pollutants, the gun. Non-violence would vastly narrow security differentials. But, in a non-violent community these narrowed differentials would be more than enough. (But a non-violent leader is at considerable risk in a violent society. I shall discuss this topic in Chapter 6).

3.   Animals have never attempted to democratise security-seeking by trying to increase the security of all members of their species - and, in some cases, even members of some or all other species. This attempt is exclusively human, and it can only be done by developing a system of collective security. The first kinds were selective and therefore divisive. For example, in protecting Jews and not Gentiles they tend to set Jews against Gentiles since hostility is soon born of unequal treatment. But security does not need to be selectively offered.

Humans have two ways of improving one another's security: through a system of alliances; and through a system of collective security. This is true of all security problems regardless of the sorts of units involved, e.g., security problems between individuals or between nations or regions. I mean to maintain that the size of the unit makes all the difference to how security should be sought, but it can only be sought through one or other of these two ways. Which one chooses depends on whether the security problem is an internal or an external one, on whether threats come from within the security organisation itself or from outside it.

When the French and Germans have gone to war every Frenchman is supposed to be the ally of any other Frenchman against any German. And so, in theory, all security problems are external, and threats are being met by instituting a totally inclusive alliance of the French against the Germans. But the worst threats to our security often come from our own kind - from moles in our secret services or from traitors in our armed services. The result is that there are sometimes internal problems of security. How can we democratise security under these circumstances? Only by forming a system of collective security - a system in which we all ally ourselves against those who disturb the peace of the system and those trouble-makers who are members of the collective security system. In theory each dispute settles anew who are friends and who are foes; and, if the system is working well, the likelihood of members of the system turning out to be friends rather than foes is always large.

A small circle of friends, A, B, C, D and E serves, in different circumstances, to illustrate both methods of security-seeking. If a bully or gang assaults one of them as they walk down the street they rush to each other's defence. In other words, they normally behave as an alliance. But now and then after they have been drinking, A and E will quarrel and even come to blows. When this happens B, C, and D do not take sides with one or other of the belligerents; they all at once attempt to separate them. They intervene to stop violence, recognising that their customary alliance has been temporarily disrupted and that a small system of collective security needs to take its place.

In what follows I shall have more to say about collective security than about alliances. One of my reasons is that although alliances can virtually eliminate security problems of certain kinds, our ultimate security problems remain since they are internal, stemming from bad faith, corruption and criminality - and these demand systems of collective security. Also, at first thought, such systems seem paradoxical. This is because the threats to their members which systems exist to meet do not come from outsiders but from their own members. It is they who are a threat to one's security; and yet it is also from them that one's security is to come. This paradox is most easily resolved at the street level of security, where we are all used to the slight gamble we take that the next human we meet will be a threat, rather than yet another source of security.

Collective security can take two forms: general systems of collective security all the members of which are supposed to help quell any outbreak of violence; and systems which have sired special organs of security, e.g., police forces, international armies, etc.

The international security system of the 1930's was intended to be of the first sort. In theory, as soon as any country was attacked by another country all member countries ganged up on the aggressor. Unfortunately, threats to security were known to be considerable and alliances had been formed to meet them. The result was that the victims of aggression only expected to be rescued by allies and not by non-allies who belonged to the general system.

Prior to the coming of such reformers as Fielding and Peel, much interpersonal security depended on people at large. Passers-by gave chase to thieves who had robbed someone, giving rise to such practices as hues and cries, sanctuary, etc. The parable of the Good Samaritan is a story of the kind of human who makes collective security possible - of the human who is prepared to intervene.

But for many reasons the collective has also found it useful to form professional agencies of security - armies and policing agencies, and also a large miscellany of private commercial organisations. Escalation - especially the advent of guns - made the price of intervention too heavy for the run of people. Law enforcement is far more effectively carried out if the worst of it, at least, is carried out by professionals. Support is made far more reliable when it is at least officered by a force of men and women who have been specially trained to provide it.

In the second kind of system, then, a body of people is assigned the special professional duty of looking after all members of the community; and of looking after them without fear or favour, protecting the poor and unpopular as readily as the rich and universally esteemed. Its success depends on the egalitarian provision of security. For example, as long as blacks get less security than whites through police support, the system is in danger of breaking down. It only thrives on a basis of strict equality: one man's tax dollar must be seen to buy as much as another's.

Chapter 3

MULTILATERALISM, UNILATERALISM AND GORBACHEV

Multilateral agreements to disarm are the obvious way of stopping escalation and actually reversing the whole mental set of the nations of the world towards one another. In many ways they already act as friends. When it comes to such things as postal services, weights and measures, and currencies, they act sensibly. But in more fundamental matters, where suspicion is profound, they act like malevolent neutrals. And only disarmament can turn them into as thorough-going friends as the various states or provinces of an efficient federation. It does this by making people more trustful. For, by and large, people only believe you don't mean to hurt when you can't hurt much anyway, whether you want to hurt or not. Defence has to shrink to a relatively small item before mutual trust brings international security. And this shrinking is possible, as Canada shows. How much would Canada spend on defence if it didn't have the rest of the world to consider? Most of the bill is like paying club membership dues. Most of Canada's international security is SAID to depend on NATO; and therefore, on what its principal members spend on security. NATO wants Canada to show some willingness to pay for the Western system of defence. And so Canadian troops aren't there to safeguard Quebecois from Ontarians. Those two groups are about as politically opposed as Canadians ever are, and yet there's not the slightest risk of Quebecers making a sudden descent on a helpless Toronto, or of a heroic Torontan force storming the Heights of Abraham. Trust is what our problem is all about. We NEED trust to make the agreement that would increase our trustfulness. No lesser price can be paid for a disarmament agreement. At best, such agreements can only be reached at a time of political thaw - and someone has to warm the atmosphere if there is to be a thaw. Someone has to thaw first. If I'm part of a knitting circle who aren't smiling at one another this season, and I'm complaining about the other unsmilers to someone who hasn't yet contracted the disease, perhaps, instead of complaining, I should be stealing myself to smile first? Someone will have to. Disarmament is just the same. Someone has to start disarming before the rest of us will agree to do so. Disarmament doesn't begin with an agreement to disarm; it begins with a unilateral act of disarmament. Nothing less will bring about political thaw, and only a political thaw makes multilateral disarmament agreements possible. Once disarmament starts it is advisable to keep it as multilateral and egalitarian as possible: equality promotes more and more mutual trust. But it is idle to suppose that it will be started off with a serious agreement to disarm. Mutual distrust is so steadily reinforced by escalation that the major powers can't agree about ending it.

The difficulty of reaching disarmament agreements is well illustrated by the 1930's when strenuous efforts were made to reach them and all manner of disarmament proposals were put forward by the Great Powers. But they were so distrustful of one another that the mere making of a proposal was enough to raise everybody's suspicions, often with justification. But it was because they trusted each other so little that they behaved so badly. Someone had to act better first, before agreements to do so could be concluded; and nobody was willing to play this unilateral role. So nothing came of it all; and the system of collective security which was supposed to be in place was almost entirely mythical.

Agreements to disarm presuppose political thaw, and political thaw presupposes unilateral concessions - concessions that show a willingness to trust others to a greater extent than they are prepared to trust you. And the concessions only make a difference when they are known to be real, i.e., known to be made at some cost in security to the conceder.

Negotiations have gone better since WW2. Some agreements that are clearly valuable to all have sometimes been reached after years, even many years, of hard bargaining. But that is the most we have been able to achieve even with only two Super Powers at the bargaining table - and generally speaking, the fewer the bargainers the more likely the agreement.

'Yes, who's fool enough to trust more than he's trusted? It's asking for trouble. And what's in it for No. 1?' Quite possibly nothing in many situations. We often make vain sacrifices. For example, we sacrifice for children who do not accept the 'benefit' of our sacrifices. Someone HAS to run the unilateral risk if we are ever to stop the armaments' race. And what ground is there for thinking that we shall be more trustful in some future year? To be the one who takes the risk does create temporary dangers. On the other hand, being the risk-taker oneself is the only way one has of making sure that SOMEONE does actually take the risk - and with so much at stake this is surely a self-serving thing to do? For the situation is one of those awkward ones in which, though it is not essential for X to take a certain step it IS necessary for that step to be taken by somebody including X. The risks of escalation are such that we are all drowned unless someone does something unilaterally - what do a few more fathoms matter?

But why suppose that others would not follow the unilateralist's lead? The concession, by causing a thaw, has made an agreement more likely than it may ever be again. It is only sense to avail yourself of that rather than to use the chance to do the conceder an injury. Treachery might bring you some booty, but it would still lose you the chance of life. But these gains are small beer compared with the advantages to be had through multilateral disarmament agreements. Defence costs are horrific and we all dread another world war. Almost all of us are LONGING for disarmament. But we refuse to disarm unless everyone agrees to disarm; and everyone is afraid to begin till someone starts the process.

Unilateralists can be radical in many different degrees. There are complete unilateralists. They favour complete military disarmament, regardless of how others behave. There are those who seek parity in some arms but have decided never to use others. For instance, some believe in the unconditional renunciation of nuclear weapons. Others again are unilateralists at home but multilateralists abroad. They think that Britain should rid itself of its own nuclear weapons, but they would urge the Americans to keep theirs. And so on. But at least unilateral proposals must involve serious concessions: otherwise they are made in vain. But what all unilateralists appreciate is this: multilateralism presupposes some substantial act of unilateralism; general concessions can be agreed to only when they have been fostered by a unilateral concession.

I now wish to apply these observations to a leader who has shown a marked capacity for doing the unprecedented: Gorbachev.

He has taken a variety of unilateral initiatives - leaving Afghanistan, reducing his armed forces, introducing glasnost, repealing Clause 6 of the Soviet constitution, and allowing communism to collapse in Eastern Europe. The reductions in his armed forces have been moderate in extent. But glasnost was the greatest unforced act of disarmament that any country has ever made. But we only appreciate this if we set out seriously to see glasnost as it must have looked to Soviet leaders, especially Gorbachev himself. Suppression, and the disinformation made possible by suppression, were the tools of power in Stalinist society: agreeing not to exercise those powers was a mammoth act of renunciation. Gorbachev's recent troubles at home themselves show this. If there had been rebels in the Caucasus and the Baltic States in Stalin's time, and that is itself highly improbable, they would not have known of one another's existence - and nor should we. And nobody would have known how brutally the rebellions had been crushed. For no regime in history has rested on as many nameless graves as Stalin's.

But even if we underrate the significance of that particular concession we cannot deny that he has shown a willingness to injure himself so as to put others into a disarmament mood. In other words, he has used unilateralism as the tool of multilateralism, gradually convincing distrust-pickled Westerners that he was no serious threat to them.

The only way of overcoming distrust is to reduce the fears that we arouse in one another. There seem to be three main ways in which this can be done: by showing yourself to be less formidable than had been supposed; by convincing your opponent of your sincere desire for reconciliation; and by showing him that the grounds of the quarrel are becoming less and less substantial. The opponent can be induced to ask any, and preferably all, of the following questions: Could he hurt me even if he tried? Does he want to hurt me? And why should I suppose that he does? - what are we quarrelling about anyway?

With astonishing skill and daring Gorbachev has used all these methods. Glasnost, as a process of national self-exposure, enabled others to see how much was amiss in the Soviet Union - how far the nation was from being fighting fit. Many things were probably going badly even in Stalin's time. But if anyone knew it - which is disputable - it was only Stalin himself. Now the whole world knows that Gorbachev is in difficulties. We all concede that the U.S.S.R. has gigantic muscles. But we now doubt whether its economic heart is strong enough to drive those muscles. And also whether, knowing that it has a weak heart, it could want it to come to driving muscles against a powerful enemy.

But Gorbachev has not only shown that he is in no shape for war: he has also shown that making war is the last thing he wants to do. He has made some military concessions. He has refused to prop up communism in Eastern Europe. He has ended the political monopoly of communism in his own country. He has shown every willingness to reach an agreement. Finally, Gorbachev's communism is getting quite a look of democracy about it - so much so that there does not seem much to fight about even if he still insists on giving his regime the bad old name of communism.

The result of all these unilateral concessions has been a much greater political thaw than has been known since World War II - a thaw that is so considerable that at the moment multilateralism actually seems possible. It is as well that this is so since Gorbachev is clearly not an undiluted unilateralist. His basic allegiance is to multilateralism. He is certainly not prepared to give up his massive nuclear weaponry till some of America's nuclear weaponry has been dismantled. He has shown himself prepared to start off the process of disarmament. But once it has been started he will expect as many concessions as he makes himself.

Chapter 4

PACIFYING THE PLANET

Disarmament is essential if humans are to survive; and now, thanks to Gorbachev, disarmament is possible. But to what point should we disarm? And what forms should disarmament take? Most of us do not look further than disarmament - and those who think that humans only repeat their mistakes do not even look so far. But it is useful NOW to look further than that, e.g., to consider what disarmament might lead to. World government? An end to security problems beyond the level of interpersonal relations? We shall never put a stop to sudden death on dark nights and in lonely corners. But could disarmament not lead to a time when large groups of humans no longer resorted to violence to settle their disputes?

1.   Can anything be said in a general way about the ideal security system? The answer is 'yes'. There are two general things that can be said about the ideal system of security, and both are of the greatest importance. These are inclusiveness, i.e., the inclusion of every person or nation or security unit which might belong to the organisation in question, and externality of security problems, i.e., having the characteristic of not being weakened by any internal security problems. In brief, the ideal of a security system is an inclusive alliance. Let me consider some examples.

The three musketeers made a great team, especially with the help of d'Artagnan. But there were plenty of people who did not belong to their team. Their security system - 'all for one and one for all' - was the best of its kind. But divisive systems which pit a few against the world are radically inferior. They externalise risk, yes. But great risks remain, as they well know. Their alliances externalise risks, certainly. But it is a big world out there, and danger may come from any part of it. That did not bother the three musketeers: trouble was their business. But it bothers ordinary human security seekers who are concerned first to clear certain spheres of risks, and then to make these spheres from which risks have been cleared as big as possible. When they include everyone or everything which could possibly be a member risks have been externalised out of existence and security problems of the kind which the system is intended to meet have been ended. If some people or things do not belong to the system and could belong to it, external risks remain - as they would have remained in Europe between the world wars after the Nazis had left the League of Nations.

But inclusiveness is not enough, as the case of German membership of the League serves to show. For even if Germany had remained a member it would have posed deadly risks for other members, bringing risks internal to the security system and converting what might have been an alliance into something weaker: a system of collective security, a system that had not wholly externalised security problems. Hence the German case shows us that the ideals of inclusiveness and externality can come into conflict.

When this occurs sometimes the one is preferred and sometimes the other, depending on circumstances. Externality of risks was clearly sacrificed for inclusiveness by the many British people in the 1930s who would rather have seen the Nazis belong to the League even though they were feared by most European countries. But, generally speaking, as risks increase, there is a growing tendency to turn to externality of risks at the price of lessening inclusiveness. For example, in countries where it is dangerous to go about alone people often travel in packs or at least in pairs. Greater dangers have driven them into forming alliances.

Systems of collective security are only effective in two sets of circumstances: when the membership is large; and when a firm alliance has fallen into temporary disrepair and has degenerated into a system of collective security.

A large membership ensures that each member can only be personally acquainted with a small part of the total membership. This means that when members meet they usually meet as strangers and are enabled to view one another ambivalently, mainly as possible sources of security to one another but also residually as possible sources of danger. If they knew one another it would be more natural for them to form potentially conflicting alliances rather than a system of collective security - a system which, if sufficiently inclusive, exists to solve the security problems among its members. The only effective systems of collective security are to be found at the street level - and even at that level they are only effective if fairly exacting conditions are met. (More will be said about these conditions later on). The attempt to institute such a system at the international level is absurd. The international scene is much like a chance assembly of neighbourhood cats: they all know each other and whose claws pose a threat. It is only sense for them to form alliances, not systems of collective security.

But the one type of system can degenerate into the other. A, B, C, D and E are a circle of firm friends. But occasionally, if they get tipsy, A and E will fall out and even come to blows. When this occurs B, C and D invariably combine to separate them, ganging up on the violent rather than taking sides. In normal times they form an alliance. But when such quarrels occur they temporarily form something inferior but still useful, i.e., a system of collective security. But in such cases the system of collective security is merely interruptive, soon giving place to the usual alliance when the emergency is over.

It follows that collective security is only possible at the level of security at which problems are tamed, not solved, i.e., at the street level. My general conclusion, then, is this: the appropriate instrument of high level security is the alliance - an inclusive alliance if possible, and a potentially divisive alliance if necessary; and the appropriate instrument of street protection is collective security.

2.   In my view, this conclusion enhances our understanding of the long-term drift towards political unification.

Changes have not all been in one direction, of course: there are also powerful forces working for greater political division. The greatest of these is nationalism - a disease that afflicts people from all walks of life and from all parts of the globe. Nevertheless, in spite of endless bigotry and short-sightedness, the world is clearly coming together. For example, customs unions have been either formed or planned in Europe, North America, South America and Asia; and customs unions have developed into single states in the past and seem likely to do so again.

Petty kingdoms marked Man's political infancy. His adolescence was the Age of Empire, the still recent times when alliances consisted mainly of subjects rather than of true allies, and the main thrust behind unification was conquest. This was a false start towards the political maturity of unification. Political giants sprawled across the earth, one of them even boasting that he always had a part of himself in the sun. But this sprawling arrogance was increasingly resented; and, as soon as they could, subject peoples set about the long-drawn-out struggles that led to their emancipation. Now, as we grow more mature, we are building up our political unions again, owing our growth not to subjugating one another but to forming marriages of convenience on a new egalitarian basis.

In some respects it is obviously convenient to be big to the point of complete inclusiveness. For example, it is useful to have a world-wide postal union. And regions sharing problems, traditions and interests are finding it best to enter into closer and closer alliances.

Federation is the usual instrument of greater unity; and it is often successful. The main dangers to it are either when it contains narrower loyalties which have priority over wider ones, or when it includes constituent parts which are too unequal in size and influence. For example, it would be a danger to the United States of America or or Europe if Danes felt that being a Dane was more important politically than being European; or if Germans attempted to command too large a share of Europe's power or wealth. But often it is successful enough to obliterate the security problems of former times.

Europe is the most promising of recent cases: ridden by war as recently as 1945, and already talking of unification four or so decades later. Of course, this process has been aided and abetted by a common fear of the Soviet Union. Nonetheless, it is remarkable. And now that Gorbachev is refusing the role of enemy who can say where the process of unification may end? There is certainly a serious prospect that the world will come together like coalescing ink blobs.

Federation obliterates ancient security problems: it also prevents the emergence of new ones. This is to be seen in the histories of the U.S.A., Canada, Australia and the Union of South Africa where large units of federal membership have stopped some kinds of security problems from ever developing. At the price of one civil war in America these federations have been able to forestall warmongering among the large states or provinces of which they are composed.

Federation reduces so many problems, as a rule, that it does not make sense not to federate once the main obstacles have been overcome. The two difficulties I have mentioned are important but not necessarily fatal to successful federation: the main obstacle lies elsewhere. It is a willingness to let quarrels escalate to the levels of organised violence. Ideally, humans should abandon this kind of violence altogether. Humanity still falls far short of this ideal. But even now there are foreigners and foreigners: it is quite permissible to kill some, if the cards fall badly, but it is no longer permissible to kill others. For example, since 1945 the British have had a 'cod-war' with Iceland. It was a serious dispute leading to shots across opponents' bows. But in 1976 it was patched up without blood-letting. When this point is reached countries can be said to be ripe for federation.

3.   Unifying the world is an advanced stage on the road to pacification, and the pacification of the planet is the ultimate goal of security-seeking. But what is it exactly? And would we have reached its limit if we managed to settle all security problems above the interpersonal level? - for what I have been saying carries the hope that pacification may reach that stage of development. The befuddled would still brawl; and political office-bearers would still steal each others' jobs and wives much as usual. But they would always prevail over hotheadedness in larger groups of people, trouble-and-warmakers always

being heavily outnumbered. This is because the great majorities would have learned to love their neighbours enough not to kill them, or even to organise to kill them if human affairs work out badly enough. All the killing still done, would be by people who would be put away for it.

'But what if - against any odds - fighting broke out in the federation?' As soon as fighting began the federation would cease to be an inclusive alliance. But, like a disrupted circle of friends, the likelihood is that it would still function as a security system - no longer as an alliance, certainly, but as an interruptive system of collective security. This is because it is probable that federal forces and wealth would be marshalled to put down the fighting - to quench wrath.

4.   'But what about tyranny, the police state and so forth? Mightn't this world state become the ultimate political monster?'

In answer to such questions I want to stress early intervention. All the usual, and some unusual, precautions should be taken, of course. For example, rulers should never be allowed to rule for long or too completely; the different functions of government should be separated; and the whole population should be taught to see tyranny as the supreme political hazard, and one that we all have a duty to thwart. It must also be insisted that in a humane and rational society a firm distinction is drawn between freedom and licence, and that no right is to be regarded as inviolable. People should certainly be free to talk hot air, but they cannot be permitted to talk treason and conspiracy. Tyranny is of enormous concern to us all: there are limits to how free we can allow speech to be when speaking has become a kind of doing. Even J.S. Mill, a lord of liberty, conceded that a free assembly may need to be dispersed when it is being goaded into acts of violence. Nothing must be allowed to interfere with the needs of early intervention - for early intervention is much our greatest safeguard against escalation. In Chapters 6 & 7 I shall be dealing with the anti-crime aspect of this question. At the moment I am restricting myself to its political aspect.

Ordinary people are the best watchdogs of political freedom; and at any price in curtailment of liberty nothing must be allowed to prevent them from doing their job. The watchdog is an intervener and early warner. If he is worth his keep he does not wait till after the burglary before he starts to bark. He can counter burglarious intent by taking off the seat of a man's trousers, but he is still better at waking his master before an entrance has been gained into his home. He prevents even better than he cures; and we should follow his example. We need to find acceptable - or, if necessary, relatively acceptable -means of intervening early before the bad has come to the worst. (Security precautions at airports are an example. Almost all of us accept their necessity even though we all recognise that they are a nuisance).

But, in spite of the best that the good citizen can do, occasionally social emergencies are likely to develop. For instance, pressure groups and parties may emerge which are capable of doing grave injury to the body politic. The American N.R.A. seems to me just such a pressure group - one which, in spite of its vociferous but nonsensical denials is responsible for a large tally of dead every single year. What should be done about it? America needs to be wooed by every committed enemy of the gun. There needs to be a countering and dedicated anti-gun lobby. This anti-gun lobby should have been brought into existence long ago. For evils should be organised against as soon as they appear; and the gun has been the curse of America from the beginning. Let me turn to a still more controversial illustration. What would have happened if Jews and concerned humans everywhere had organised in opposition to Hitler and his fellow gangsters the moment that Mein Kampf appeared? They may not have been able to stop him. He was naturally gifted at the rascalities of politics and he had many important factors working in his favour. But I myself believe that he could have been stopped before he had properly started - and that that was the proper time to have stopped him. I am not showing wisdom after the event: I am pleading for early intervention. Surely that is what the need for dedicated parental care is all about? - the need to steer the talented Adolf in a very different direction. The nursery is society's first attempt at early intervention. We do intervene early already. But we do it half-heartedly, not really believing that we can make much difference to the world, as Hitler's father probably did. Early intervention is the only shortcut to utopia - as winning a lottery is the poor man's only short cut to wealth. Long odds are generally accepted in the latter case, why not in the former?

No, I have not given detailed answers to the questions with which I have been dealing. But general answers are often the best means we have of curbing political extremism. Humans habitually defeat their own ends by running to extremes - and this is true, above all, of freedom-lovers.

Chapter 5

THE MORAL WEAPON

So far I have claimed that human security-seeking has been innovative in two fundamental ways, one bad - escalation of weaponry, and one good - the democratisation of security-seeking through the institution of alliances and collective security; the one a flowering of moral agency, and the other a blighting of the species that must end in its extinction if it is allowed to continue unchecked. But humans have also been innovative in a still more fundamental way: they have devised a 'weapon' that at last matches their ultimately moral and spiritual nature, the weapon that Gandhi, beyond comparison its greatest user, called 'the non-violence of the strong'. This third fundamental innovation is - as I hope to show - so intimately connected with the second, i.e. with collective security, that collective security would reach peak effectiveness only in a world of convinced believers in non-violence. This is because the efficiency of a collective security system depends on factors which are steadily reinforced as the world is pacified or grows less violent.

'How can you use the word 'weapon' of something that makes a point of weaponlessness?' Because - as was pointed out by Richard Gregg more than half-a-century ago - non-violence is like jujitsu: it turns their own violence on the violent. This is exactly what happened to Ceaucescu: the armed might which he hoped to turn on the people was turned on him - and the weaponry which slew the tyrant was provided by him.

We do not know how long the moral weapon has been developing - certainly for immensely longer than the beginnings of recorded history since there are gestures towards morality even in animal behaviour. What we do know is that this weapon has been getting stronger and stronger, sharper and more reliable, where the run of ORDINARY people are concerned.

This story of progress is not uniform, of course. From time to time there have been setbacks of a truly ghastly kind, e.g., the Jewish holocaust and two world wars. But it is only necessary to read Sir Norman Angell's book *The Great Illusion* to realise that enormous gains have been made in living memory. The widespread revulsion against the useless slaughter of the Falkland and Gulf Wars are only two of many recent examples.

Nearly all humans respond morally in one degree or another. But some - still many? - do not respond enough to provide the necessary basis for a moral weapon. They would not turn their guns on a tyrant till the next man, and the next, had turned their guns on him, and he is as good as buried. They can do the right thing at last - given a sufficiency of good examples. Others are quick to respond in a positive way to the calls of need and suffering, to cries for help. I believe that they now constitute the majority of any normal modern community.

Admittedly things can go so amiss politically as to damp down the moral responsiveness of a whole community, as the Nazis damped down the moral responsiveness of the Germans. But there is a limit to this unresponsiveness even when it has been damped down. For example, Hitler and his gang only temporarily blunted the moral sensibilities of the Germans: most of the hearts that used to beat under Nazi uniforms were as warm as those of their enemies, and this warmth could have been turned against the tyrant. That only fatigue would have stayed the homocidal frenzy of Hitler and a minority of his followers I have no doubt whatsoever. But I also believe that the majority could have been induced to disobey him. Ceaucescu was only a smaller Hitler who did not know when to self-destruct. If Hitler had lived longer he too would have been swept aside by a hurricane of disobedience.

In my chapter on planetary pacification I suggested that this supremely benign process might be carried to its limit without anyone having renounced violence unilaterally. Unilateral actions are needed at the beginning of this process: the Gorbachev role is indispensable. But once it has been played and the process of disarmament has commenced what point is there in further unilateralism? - especially the extreme kind that is involved in placing one's trust in the non-violence of the strong? I myself have suggested that pacification might occur without further help from unilateralists, including believers in non-violence. Since such stands are not clearly necessary are they even beneficial? This is the general question behind what follows.

1.   How does the new weapon relate to the earlier ones? The most fundamental of the differences between them is that the new weapon cannot be used to kill. Worse, in many people's eyes, is the fact that it does not even make it physically harder for someone to kill you. It CAN be used to defend - but only causes, not flesh and blood. However, what it cannot defend it DOES protect.

It would be fanciful to see non-violent protection as the descendant of the colour protection that is used by zebras and others to gain security. But it does make it harder for you to be seen by your enemies. You are not drawing attention to yourself by posing a threat: you are ignorable because harmless. And even when - perhaps because you are disobeying orders - you do attract attention, your conduct is of a kind that calms both humans and animals: anger-quelling friendliness and calmness, an absolute refusal to be driven to extremes, regardless of enemy actions.

Animals do not appear to show respect for other animals, except (at most) by avoiding them. They seem to be dedicated to the hierarchical viewpoint. And so they left it to Man, the only moral agent in our world, to discover egalitarianism and to develop the respectful eye of equality.

In my view, committing oneself to non-violence is the final stage on the road to according full respect to other moral agents. It brings one to the point where, sooner than eliminate them, one is prepared to put oneself at their mercy. Atrocities may ensue. But only one side will be responsible for these atrocities; and the continuing harmlessness of the other will put a brake on their opponents, first slowing their rush into mindless savagery and then inducing them to listen to the voice of justice. Sometimes one's opponent's conscience responds quickly to moral appeals; sometimes years of struggle are needed, as they were needed to dislodge the British from India. But if resisters are persistent in their purpose and in their non-violence it is very probable that the injustice at issue will be substantially remedied and that the two sides will be partially or wholly reconciled.

Submission and dominance cannot be regarded as the ancestors of egalitarianism, but they provide us with the best reasons why it needed to be born.

As Gandhi was often at pains to explain, the non-violence of the strong is very different from the non-violence of the weak. The non-violence of the weak is the non-violence of submission. But the non-violence of the strong is the non-violence of those who are prepared to resist to the death but who are not prepared to kill in the course of their resistance. Their spirit is quite different from that of the submissive wolf. They resemble him in having exposed their jugulars. But the wolf does it to demonstrate its complete domination by another wolf: the man does it as moral agent to moral agent, appealing to the other's conscience - though also applying the pressures of non-violent sanctions.

Non-violence is an essential principle of any mature ethic. As humans advance towards moral maturity, more and more of them will find killing in battle as intolerable as killing in the arena. For the non-violence of the strong is the only weapon that is really suited to the nature of a human being.

The more it is used, the stronger it becomes; and the more people there are in the world who are open to its firm but harmless methods of persuasion. People do not budge easily because they object strenuously to being forced. But ever increasingly they are willing to listen to the voice of justice once it has been quite purged of threats.

2.   We think of the world as being violent - and by comparison with what we want it certainly is. As St. Thomas à Kempis once put it: 'All men love peace, but few men love the things that make for peace'. Nevertheless, calling it a violent world is like saying that it always rains on Sundays. The truth is that horribly violent as the world is, it is a preponderantly non-violent world. We quarrel often and some of our quarrels escalate into world-shaking horrors. But most of us are not quarrelsome and do, as our usual practice, make a point of settling disputes as least bloodily as possible. We do not want to kill when we quarrel: increasingly, we want quarrelling to proceed along prescribed

constitutional lines- or, at worst, to remain non-violent. Non-violence is so much the rule that even the most violent have some experience and expertise in the use of at least the lower forms of non-violence, i.e., the forms which belong to the ordinary give and take of everyday transactions.

We need to rid ourselves of the myths that non-violence is rare and even outlandish: in fact, even the non-violence of the strong is a familiar phenomenon, and we all believe in its strength till much escalation has occurred and both sides have become prepared to carry their quarrel to violent extremes. It is only when we are determined to enforce if we cannot persuade that we abandon non-violence.

For millenia enforcing at the international level has proved disastrous. But people will not abandon it. They refuse to think well of their opponents once a quarrel has escalated into a fighting matter. And so they insist that enforcement is imperatively needed. 'Agreed, it didn't prove a good idea on all those other occasions. But this one is different. Above all, this one is Hitler and his gang of thugs' - and Hitler is the man most likely to scare the non-violence out of anybody.

All that is really in dispute where non-violence is concerned is whether it should be merely the usual arbiter or whether it should also be the final arbiter. Sadly, it is the case that many feel that limitless violence has to be kept in reserve - to be used if all else fails. But for an ever-growing minority of humans the last resort is non-violent resistance. This is because they are convinced not only that non-violent action is the only civilised weapon but that OVERALL and in the long run it is also much the most effective - especially in reaching just settlements rather than simply what the more determined party happens to want.

Why is it that, although most of us are agreed that non-violence pays at the lowers levels of escalating quarrels, we suppose that a different rule applies after further escalation? As usual, it probably has several roots. The first is that until much escalation has occurred our quarrels have frameworks and we believe that recognised procedures exist for settling them. I suspect that we conclude from this that when disputants remain non-violent they do so because an authority exists to whom their disputes can be referred. This is often true - so much so that it is vital to establish more such authorities. But it is surely false to suppose that violence becomes the usual arbiter when quarrels erupt and there is no recognised person or body to whom they can be referred? It is doubtful whether this was true even in primitive times: today it is wildly wide of the mark. Again, we are much too apt to think of quarrels as total - in spite of the fact that even wars have never been total, since belligerents have never engaged in violence which takes absolutely no account of previously acknowledged conventions and agreements. This is as true of the Nazis as of all other recent malefactors.

A third root is that we often take black-and-white views of conflicts, refusing to credit our opponents with having even a crutch to stand on - and this in spite of the mammoth historical improbability of right being wholly on one side.

But our persistent faith in arms is also due to absurd notions about enforcement itself. The first of these errors is also the greatest, namely, the error of supposing that enforcement is always possible. A country can be beaten to its knees as India was prior to the coming of Gandhi, and it can then abandon arms and rid itself of its oppressors without killing any of them. It has often been said that Gandhi had especially easy opponents in the British - the only jolly good chaps ever to build an empire. But the truth was that the British were, and are, so used to feeling morally superior that to be made to feel that they were in the wrong, was something that they must be expected to be stubborn about. But in the end, efforts at enforcement were exposed for the short-sighted nonsense they are. Even the old proverb knows better: 'You can lead a horse to water but you can't make it drink'. Even mediaeval torture chambers did not invariably intimidate their victims: in all ages heroic men and women have refused to be cowed by any degree of violence and cruelty.

The second error is to forget that wars not only have to be won, they also have to be used to gain the ends for which they were fought. Not only can those ends still be frustrated by the 'beaten' enemy: the victors can lose the will to give political shape to their military triumph. And it is easy to think that winning the war was fight enough without having to win the peace as well. And so many a tale of victory has turned into a story of defeat. History does not end with the sound of victory bells: it did not in 1945, and no other year will be any different.

Non-violence might have been used as a last as well as a first resort if women had become the bigger spiders in the human web. Certainly, men have been responsible for the great bulk of homicides. This worries some women and they still hope to catch up. Fortunately, the great majority of the once gentler sex remains comparatively gentle. Relative physical weakness encourages the use of both kinds of non-violence - that of the strong as well as the weak. It forges the weapons of guilt and deceit. But it also forges the weapon of satyagraha. Women have been past mistresses of guile and deceit, as any courtesan well knows. But they have also been past mistresses of satyagraha, challenging the strong without weapons and with much wit.

It is wrong to call the non-violence of the strong 'the Womanly Way'. For in spite of men's bloody record some men have used the moral weapon with consummate skill and conviction. It is not the Womanly Way: it is the Humanly Way.

3.   Non-violent sanctions

'Lysistrata' strongly hints that non-violent sanctions have been used by humans from the beginnings of history. Economic sanctions are also very ancient. For example, in early wars combatants often laid waste their own property and lands rather than allow them to fall into the hands of the enemy. This was not only bloody-mindedness: they knew that if aggressors are denied their spoils there will be less aggression. In a time of chronic shortage they would never have resorted to such extremes if they had not been convinced that they were of vital strategical importance. The Gulf War might be taken as a counter example since economic sanctions were first tried and are supposed to have met with little success. But there are many reasons for disputing any negative conclusion about economic sanctions. In the first place, Bush was impatient, knowing that he could not leave an army just standing on sentry duty in the desert. He could not wait for economic sanctions to have their desired results. Also, military reverses are hard to disguise. Gains and losses are usually visible and are often recorded. But economic drains, the bleeding to death of a whole society which is brought about by economic sanctions, are much easier to disguise. Strategists have to work in deeper twilight since it is often impossible to tell whether one is gaining ground - let along gaining it decisively. This is one of the disadvantages of non-violent methods: good judgment depends on more imagination, intelligence, foresight and patience than are indispensably required for good military judgment.

I now propose to diverge very briefly from my argument in order to deal with the case which is usually seen as the chief obstacle in the path of those who advocate the use of non-violence: the Hitler case.

In my own view Hitler is no special hurdle for the non-violent. It is probable that he would have been defeated by non-violent methods of resistance far more quickly and less bloodily than he was by Eisenhower and the Russians. His profound brutality would have been at once exposed if his opponents had used non-violent methods - assuming that he was obeyed initially, and was therefore allowed to give free expression to his own nature. He told us in Hitlerian language what he would have done to Gandhi and his followers, if he had ever had to deal with them - and I believe every word of what he said, as far as his own intentions were concerned. Man proposes and God disposes. Similarly, tyrants propose and the downtrodden masses sometimes dispose. For tyrants are only as strong as the power of mass obedience - and the limitedness of such obedience is well attested. This power of obedience is soon sapped by the extremes of brutality. It would have been precisely Hitler's nastiness that would have made non-violent resistance - the moral weapon - effective against him. For Germans Hitler was the man who had cocked a snook at enemy opinion and had put an end to the injustices of Versailles. It felt good to be feared again after all those years of being slighted and badly treated. And one could not be SURE that the talk of death camps was well-founded. Hitler's Germany did not seem such a ghastly place, seen from an Aryan's perspective. But non-violent resistance would have been opposed so brutally that Hitler would have been revealed to his followers as the satanic human he undoubtedly was. He would have mown down unarmed people, and those who objected to it would have been mown down themselves. But making an example of people is not only frightening, it fuels revolt. If unbridled intimidation is resorted to, as it would have been if Hitler had had Gandhi to contend with, the point would soon have been reached when brave souls would have burst into view all over the place and a foul regime would have been swept away by a massive wave of disobedience. His brutality is a despot's strength, up to an undetermined point: beyond that point - beyond the obedience barrier - it is his undoing.

The Hitler case had to be confronted somewhere or other in this short book, and this seemed as good a place to confront it as any. Of course, I have been brief and sweeping, as was to be expected when the Hitler case is not my main subject. But I believe that it would have been possible to give an adequate answer that boiled down to what I have said.

The power of economic sanctions rests on economic dependencies, and these come in all sizes, from the stranglehold that the U.S.S.R. probably has on Lithuania to the barely perceptible pressure that Greenland might exert on Denmark. Some economic sanctions could do little harm: others are potentially ruinous. And when Mrs. Thatcher used to say that economic sanctions on South Africa were useless she herself was well aware that the loss of her South African trade was injurious to Britain.

'But is it morally permissible for a non-violent country to resort to economic sanctions. Isn't it potentially too harmful - at least in some cases?'

Strikers who are often ready to exploit any form of economic dependence have frequently been challenged by such questions. They are asked: 'Aren't you damaging your country's vital exports by shutting down your car plant? Aren't you, as a doctor or nurse, condemning innocents to death if you withold your services?' Except in those cases where the law has curtailed the right to strike because of the damage which a strike might do, strikers have seldom shown much reluctance to exploit a dependence.

It should be quite different with non-violent resisters, if they are worthy of the moral weapon which they claim to be using: their methods have to look morally acceptable to those on whom they are used. Your opponents must see you as a responsible, caring and rational agent - the only truly appropriate user of the moral weapon.

What I mean can be well illustrated from Gandhi's long struggle, a struggle in which he showed again and again that he was a suitable user of that weapon. He acted as a moral agent, not as a run-of-the-mill striker.

Using a moral weapon is like appealing to Caesar. If you appeal to Caesar you are liable to be taken to him - at which time it would be well for you to have something clear and good to say for yourself. Your sovereign foes will be your judges. And the effectiveness of your non-violence will depend on how well you stand up their scrutiny.

This means that you will be chivalrous in your use of economic sanctions, not making the most of them when times are hard for your opponent. For example, when times were hard for Britain in WW2 Gandhi called off a satyagraha campaign, refusing to take advantage of the Japanese threat to British India. And I believe that this refusal to exploit a favourable situation caused a deep wound in the collective conscience of the British Establishment, opening its eyes to the enormity of such notions as that of 'subject peoples' and all the glory-mongering of imperialism. It affected their basic attitudes, ensuring that Nkrumah and others had a much easier time of it than Gandhi.

The very best non-violent practice can be reduced to St. Augustine of Hippo's famous dictum: 'Love, and do what you like'.

4.   It was once said of the Scottish hero, William Wallace, that only he was man enough to wield his giant sword. This saying draws attention to a paradoxical feature of the moral weapon: although it takes a giant to put it to the best use, we are all strong enough to make some use of it. The 'all-edged sword', as Gandhi called it, is never more healing than when it wounds: it blesses its user and also him on whom it is used. Even those who might seem specially unsuited to its use, e.g., those trained in violence and the extremes of obedience, have sometimes made excellent use of non-violent methods. The best illustrations of this have perhaps been provided by the warlike followers of Badshar Khan on the North West frontier of India. One's past can certainly hinder a human's use of non-violence. It does not help to have been unloving, dishonourable or pig-headed. But it must also be remembered that where morality is concerned any moment can be the start of a new life. Non-violence makes Wallaces of us all. But some Wallaces are more equal than others. For the all-edged sword is simultaneously the most aristocratic and the most democratic of weapons, drawing freely on the special gifts of the aristocrat but at the same time marginalising superiority - recognising it ungrudgingly and passing on to the problems

of ordinary people and how to make the best use of their talents. As much as anything, it draws attention to how much the aristocrat and commonplace humans need one another. Gandhi practised satyagraha supremely well. But the weapon he refurbished was used effectively by tens of millions of ordinary people. It can make good use of paragons. But you do not need to be a paragon to use it. Applying the best side of yourself is enough.

Non-violence can be spontaneous or organised; and it can be effective even when it has not been organised, as was recently shown in Rumania. Violence, on the other hand, is most unlikely to be effective unless it is organised. But organised non-violence is also much more effective. In brief, it is much better to be intentionally unarmed - to have the good fortune to be non-violent, not the bad luck to be unable to be anything else.

Why is non-violence often so impressive? What are the qualities about it which have such a marked effect on one's opponents? The most important are probably charity conjoined with harmlessness, and fearlessness. Harmlesssness encourages generosity of mind; we all feel that we can afford to be generous to the harmless. It has been seen as contemptible, of course. But only by philosophers and other incorrigible theorists: the run of pragmatic agents are only too happy to meet with it. And some of the dissenters would think again if they interpreted 'harmlessness' comprehensively enough. But harmlessness is never seen as contemptible when it is accompanied with fearlessness. Even the fearlessness of an infant who does not know any better is vaguely impressive.

Gandhi emphasised fearlessness even more than courage. To be effective the non-violent must stand firm. But most of us are afraid of standing firm - if, for instance, what we have to stand firm against is a cavalry charge. But the satyagrahi, Gandhi implied, should aim at the higher state in which she and he not only put their lives on the line but cease to be worried about what may happen to them. Not all non-violent resisters are theists, and so not all of us can say, 'I'm putting us all in God's hands'. But that is the form of words that comes naturally to me when I am thinking of this calm acceptance of whatever may befall. This is the non-violent ideal. It was also one of the things that made Gandhi so deeply impressive. From his early South African campaigns to the moment when he accepted his own death and bowed his forgiveness to his assassin, Gandhi's conduct was always an absolute model of fearlessness.

Shakespeare means us to be impressed by the followers of young Fortinbras. This is because they are willing to shed their lives like snakes shed skins even though they have not grown other ones to replace them. And this fearless facing up to the worst that can befall, does seem to function as a final test of one's humanity. If so, great non-violent resisters all pass this exalted test.

An evident and pervasive attachment to the truth is also impressive. The boyhood friend who impressed me most was the one who showed greatest honesty of mind. My family was a very honest one. But I at once recognised that I had not previously met so much of this kind of honesty. Also, I have always found that people are impressed by any surpassing honesty and integrity. Hence the perennial appeal of Regulus.

In his first Indian campaign Gandhi was acting as the peasant's advocate. (He was a lawyer). In his talks with them he always stressed that although they were very unjustly treated they must not add a jot or hair to the injustices that were being done to them. They must not exaggerate - even though they had so little to exaggerate about. The treatment one receives could always be worse.

Pervasive truthfulness and a sense of justice clearly go together: the just-minded, generally speaking, are also the honest-minded. So when Gandhi restrained the peasants from exaggerating he also had in mind to restrain them from asking for too much. You can ask for too little as well as too much, of course. In Gandhi's view, the best thing to aim at initially is minimal justice, the least you can receive without feeling resentful about it. Further adjustments are usually needed. Full justice often comes in stages, and it only comes more slowly if one gets impatient.

Resisters should avoid outraging opponents by asking for manna from heaven. Egalitarian settlements eventually emerge, if one keeps up non-violent pressure. Wearing away a stone sounds like a slow way of getting things done. But if one wants things to stay done it is often much faster than going to war about it. Hammering away at injustice, even when it seems unavailing, is also impressive. Persistence is a greatly underrated shaper of history. And it works all the greater wonders for being comparatively rare. Persistence makes one formidable. One becomes compass-like: one points and keeps pointing while others are idly cancelling their own efforts by swinging between options. 'Try, try and try again' is an achiever's refrain; and also the very hall mark of the good non-violent resister. Gandhi also shines in this respect. What could be more impressive than to go knock-knocking at closed doors, year after year, decade after decade; and then, at last, about thirty years later, to have those doors voluntarily opened?

The materials from which the moral weapon is forged, are of enormous strength. Brought together, they tend to multiply one another's power, producing an amalgum that opponents find hard to resist. This was well brought out by Sir Richard Attenborough's film, 'Gandhi', the story of Gandhi's career as a peacemaking non-violent resister. Moral greatness is a supremely attractive theme, if it can be convincingly portrayed; and Attenborough was superbly served by Ben Kingsley. The film could have been called 'The Moral Weapon'.

6.   Since it is a weapon for all seasons and conditions of humans, non-violent resistance can dispense with training and preparations, if it has to. But obviously, it is much better if resisters have made preparations and have trained themselves for the use of non-violence. It is supremely the 'make-do' weapon. It can make good use of all the advantages and qualities one can muster. But, if need be, it can also dispense with them all. One never absolutely needs more than one has.

Once your eye has been opened to the power of non-violence the pages of history are filled with cases in which some form of non-violent action by one human, a few, or many acting together, has (or have) turned the scales in matters of great importance. And these doers and sayers, the people who turned the scales, have seldom been paragons. No miracles overtake the man of violence. Life is not like one of those Japanese films in which a single samurai makes war on all the visible world and still triumphs. Numbers always count, though not always more than anything else. They are of value to the non-violent too. As a single resister, getting thrown off a South African train, Gandhi could do little. But when he persuaded his countrymen to burn their pass books the authorities had to reckon with him. On the other hand, in auspicious circumstances, a single non-violent witness to a truth can change the world. This is sometimes true even of those who suffer initial defeat, as is illustrated by the case of Galileo.

The moral weapon is always used directly and indirectly: directly on the British in Gandhi's Indian campaigns; but indirectly too, on the consciences of men and women all over the planet. At one time its indirect power was small. Your actions came to the notice of few people. But now a wide world pays attention to how you quell a riot or to what a prominent rebel thinks of you. For example, there are multitudes of people in all the continents who know that Nelson Mandela wants economic sanctions against South African to be continued until apartheid has been completely demolished. You may be able to avoid the bar of your own conscience, but you will not be able to avoid the bar of world opinion. 'Does that matter?' The answer is: yes - and increasingly yes. For it affects all manner of things, especially trade and the worth of alliances. It follows that the moral weapon has yet another distinctive feature: it strikes at all those who hear of its use and not just at immediate opponents. For example, the Soviet action against Lithuania in 1991 has endangered much economic assistance to the U.S.S.R.

The Battle of Waterloo could only be won in a single place: if it was won there, it was won everywhere. Once war is joined those who are fighting it have less and less time to give to neutral opinion. Winning is what matters to them. If you win you are sure that neutrals will soon get over their scruples. Being nice to winners usually counts for more than whether you think well of them. But the moral weapon operates differently. Gandhi used it to strike at the British conscience. But in striking at the British conscience he also struck at consciences all over the globe, giving the British some degree of a bad press wherever newspapers were sold - and especially in the U.S.A.

It is possible to plan and train for both the direct and the indirect impact of non-violent resistance: the indirect, by making the world as well informed as possible on the relevant issues; the direct, in many different ways.

A person's entire life may come to be seen as preparation and training for a subsequent career as a non-violent resister, all her long years of moral development seeming to be needed to make her achievements possible. All sorts of things can set us on our way to becoming better non-violent resisters. For example, initially we may come under the influence of an exceptional older person. But later in life self-discipline should take most of the place given earlier to discipline, to precept and to example.

The moral weapon is honed by information. People at large and everywhere cannot know too much about the subject of a dispute and how it has been conducted. And so a _satyagrahi_ is very concerned about what it is now usual to call 'propaganda'. But I object to this word on account of its latter day overtones. The _satyagrahi_ wants people to know, not to be induced - or worse, deceived - into accepting something more convenient than the truth. He thinks that the facts tell in favour of his own conception of justice. But if they do not he still wants them to come to light as they may have a bearing on the conclusion of an equitable agreement. He sees his view of the matter under dispute as only a first approximation to equity. Ideally, the _satyagrahi_'s standpoint is: 'Let justice be done - and the heavens are never less likely to fall than when we are doing it'.

Preparations for a campaign include much education, at home and abroad, the aim being to raise the world's consciousness on the disputed issue. It is also important that their followers should cease to see campaign leaders as remote figures. This can be done in many ways, far more easily now than ever before thanks to television. Gandhi did it by taking giant walkabouts which took him on rounds of thousands of Indian villages. At all times he tried to turn the title of 'Mahatma' into the very different title of 'bapu' - 'daddy'. These enormous hikes also brought him a closer knowledge of his country than was possessed by any other 20th century revolutionary; and this knowledge was of the greatest service to him in his struggle.

This mutual acquaintance of leaders and followers is also vital in military contexts, as no reader of Julius Caesar's writings is ever likely to forget. But it is probably still more important that non-violent leaders and followers should get as close as possible to one another. These close relations should bring out both the ordinariness and the extraordinariness of non-violent leaders. Ideally, such relations make leaders' gifts rather like those of a son's or daughter's - gifts which reflect too favourably on oneself to give rise to much envy.

What about the quasi-military training given to non-violent resisters at various times and places? It undoubtedly helps to hold rehearsals and to make detailed contingency plans, since we are all better off for knowing what we have let ourselves in for. Such methods are not needed to produce great satyagrahis but they certainly help to produce reliably good ones.

Nevertheless, it is still worth asking ourselves: do they wholly become a wielder of the moral weapon? For example, resisters have often been taught the postures which best save us from physical injury. Is this good practice? Or would it be better if they did nothing to protect themselves? My answer is that it makes sense to protect oneself in any way that does not blunt one's moral weapon. This means that one has to allow for differences of time and place. For example, it is possible that in America one would be credited with good sense, not cowardice, if one shields oneself from brutal people. But in India, in Gandhi's time, it may (or may not) have been different. It would have been different if satyagrahis learnt by experiment that such practices muffled the blow which they could strike with the moral weapon.

7.   'But why, after the pacification that you write about so optimistically in Chapter 4, are you pessimistic enough to see non-violence as essential? At most you show it to be merely beneficial'.

The most general point to be made in answer to this criticism is that if the beneficial is sufficiently beneficial it is also practically indispensable - and that is the essence of what I wish to claim.

To begin with, will we ever be really safe from some escalation-renewing lunacy somewhere or other till people see and believe that power does not necessarily grow out of the barrel of a gun? It can, of course; and frequently has. But the power is usually short-term, and it only exists if we allow it to do so. Mao's saying is little more than unthinking cynicism, and I believe that he must now be blushing in the shades for the political naivety which it manifested. Once we have grasped the nature of power we are proof against the obsessive belief in the special efficacy of violence.

Unilateralism was needed to set us on the road to disarmament. Similarly unilateralism is needed to set us on the road to lasting pacification. Only the out-and-out non-violent can hasten the day when fighting occurs mainly in sleazy bars, not slaughterous battlefields. Non-violent methods are overwhelmingly the best. Surely those who have reached this conclusion are obliged to get further evidence in its support by acting on it?

If we survive, the peaceful will eventually reduce violence to mere spirits - induced animality, to bare fisticuffs. 'The meek shall inherit the earth' - nothing is more certain, given that homo sapiens continues to survive and his earthly home remains biologically tolerable. But how soon the higher security problems are settled depends on ourselves: the conquest of war takes place in the human mind. For example, humans do not need to be taught by television, day after day, that the only thing that really settles disputes is a gun. They do not need to be encouraged to believe that Napoleon and Hitler were great men. They do not need to be dragged up morally, with few people caring a rap what lessons life is rubbing into them. We could tend our minds to degrees that legislators still starve of attention.

8.	In the matter of supporting evidence, non-violence suffers from the same handicaps as the women's movement. Women not only want their proper share of what the world has to offer: they also want to show that their talents entitle them to that share. But this is often hard for them to do because, until recently, even women were scarcely looking to see what women could do. Apart from Joan of Arc and a few others the more military spirits among women have been fortunately wasted - if we survive the worst that men have done we shall be doing well. But, in spite of scoffing males and other discouragements, some women at some place and time have usually proved their sex's point: that they are equally gifted and equally versatile. Nevertheless, the evidence is often hard to find. And so with the non-violent. They have been winning and winning down the centuries, but nobody has been keeping score. Victories have been like victories won by women; the merest flukes and essentially misleading guides to human affairs. In a word, they do not really count. Power is expected to grow out of the barrel of a gun. And so we do not trouble to make serious comparisons between violence and non-violence. We prefer to go on giving credence to the ancient myth that given sufficient military force one can settle anything.

I have tried to bring out the wrong-headedness of this view. Governments propose, but - if they have a mind to - people dispose, as is shown when the military power one thought that one had is frozen into immobility by spontaneous non-violent action. You can have your sword knocked from your hand: you can also put it up, as Jesus counselled Peter to do at the time of his arrest.

One way or another the warrior is a born loser. The sooner he fades away the sooner we can get on with the serious business of curbing the growth of population and of cleaning up the planet.

Non-violence is underrated largely because we refuse to notice that wars are being lost when we have sacrificed so much to win them. How can we be wrong about war when we have poured so many lives and so much treasure into winning one? What we need to look at are eventual and lasting results: we prefer to gloat over what is revealed by the Very light of the battlefield. It produced a sudden glare, certainly. But the intense darkness which follows its extinction is the time when we delightedly turn from everything connected with a war, especially its aims - and that is the beginning of defeat. The cause of country after country is supposed to have been lost in war. But the wars settled nothing which was not gradually getting settled anyway. The causes not favoured by the victors in war have triumphed again and again. In the longer run of the centuries what violence accomplishes is piffling compared with what is accomplished by peaceful methods - and refusing to fight is the first and greatest thing that any of us can do to get this truth finally recognised.

9.   Curiously enough, though there are people interesting themselves in Gandhi's ideals, and even applying them, all over the world, those who have used them have tended to omit the very thing to which Gandhi attached special importance: constructive work. Thanks to Joan Bondurant more than to anyone else, we now have detailed analyses of Gandhi's methods: his campaigns have been picked over by scholarly minds. And all would agree with what I have said about Gandhi's own emphasis. Of course, he was mortal and made mistakes - as he was always the first to admit. But we cannot value a man's work without valuing his sense of priorities; and Gandhi's view was always that constructive work should receive special attention.

        Constructive work is not part of one's preparations for non-violence: rather, it is part of one's actual campaign. Non-violent resistance can take many forms. The best known of living exponents of it, Gene Sharp, has distinguished just under two hundred of them. Gandhi saw that all such campaigning is negative. It consists of nothing except resistance. And he held that no wielder of the moral weapon should ever be content with mere resistance. Something more positive was to be expected from those who had appealed to the Caesar of justice.

        Constructive work is the title that Gandhi gave to this something-more-positive, the something which accompanies the resistance.

As I understand it, the users of the moral weapon are never prepared to use it in a wholly negative way, i.e., as an instrument of resistance. They use it to resist, certainly. But their plans are not held up while their opponents continue to frustrate them: they adjust their plans, and then do as much to implement them as can be done in a situation in which resistance must be their main task. They feel that their quest for a better society should always be expressing itself, even when their opponents are doing their best to thwart them. And so the resisters also carry out tasks which seem likely to contribute to their eventual goal. If they chose to do something which their opponents would attempt to stop it would only extend the number of disputed issues without achieving any positive result. And so the constructive work they set out to do is of kinds that their opponents are willing to permit. Ultimately, then, as I interpret it, constructive work is a means of evading one's opponents and continuing to go about one's business in the teeth of opposition. One's opponents are using violence to stop some of the things that one wants. But they are not using violence to stop all the things that one wants. And so one makes a start with tasks which will need to be accomplished. This is like beginning to win the war while battles are still being fought.

Needless to say, Gandhi's own practice corresponded with what he taught. Even his earliest campaigns have positive features. And later, in India, satyagrahis gave their attention to many useful tasks: sanitation, civil engineering works, literacy and consciousness-raising projects. And Gandhi was surely right in placing his emphasis where he did? The picking-yourself-up and getting on with it, which lie behind constructive work, are both a test and a proof of sincerity, persistance and buoyancy. They make resisters look genuine acceptable wielders of the moral weapon. The more they engage in constructive work, the more convincing and unstoppable they seem to their opponents.

Finally, constructive work sustains the membership of a non-violent movement by providing it with work and reinforcing its togetherness and conviction.

10.   I have been advocating non-violent methods of social action. But I have only been advocating them as a last resort, not a first resort.

There are fashions in almost everything, even in methods of social action; and non-violent resistance has become quite popular and modish in some quarters. Sensible movements are taking to it almost as easily as foolish movements are taking to terrorism. On the whole, this is a gratifying development. If it continues it will be a stride towards rationality and humanity. But politically, though not morally, it is often every bit as ill-considered. This is because it is socially vital not to break the law, if it is possible to avoid it: law-abidingness is a prominent feature of any reasonably good society. And how can we know whether law-breaking can be avoided if we do not exhaust the use of constitutional methods before taking to some form of civil disobedience?

Environmental groups have dissociated themselves from such dangerous (and essentially violent) practices as tree spiking. But parties of alleged environmentalists are said to have resorted to such practices. They appear to have been driven to extremes by understandable frustration: their causes are usually unexceptionable, and yet the general public blatantly continues its headlong rush to destruction. But taking to illegal practices is not the way to stop that rush while legal remedies have yet to be tried. Admittedly, you get more publicity if you are sent to prison than if you hold a peaceful and legal vigil. But if you are disposed to sigh over this loss I can only point out that you would get still more publicity if you took to killing people - or even yourselves. Caring people should not give pride of place to gaining publicity. They are particular even about publicity. They would rather not be heard about, than heard about doing the wrong things.

As might be expected, Shakespeare penned the most eloquent of the tributes that have been paid to reputation; and it deserved every bit of it. Reputation can make and break; and although one does not always get as good a reputation as one deserves, deserving a good reputation is still the best means of getting one.

People are only worsened and made more obstinate by bullying, and by those who try to bully. They respond much more favourably to wooing. And how can protesters woo the public? By continuing to tell them the plain facts about the matters at issue, and also by coming to be seen, not as a trendy nuisance, but as people who are clearing up the world for all of us. For example, I read recently of an environmental group which drew attention to a serious and illegal pollution that had been completely overlooked by the authorities. This is just the kind of thing which is wanted.

And so - summing up - my general advice to non-violent protesters would be: 'Less civil disobedience and more constructive work'.

Certainly, there are times when it is any good human's part to be a nuisance, a lawbreaker, a pest to the run of ordinary folk. Some things have to be opposed to the limits of non-violent action, not only by breaking the law but by drawing the attentions of officials to your offence. But such steps are only justified when the matter at issue is of the greatest importance and all legal methods have failed.

The non-violence I have been recommending is a substitute for extremes of violence. It is the final arbiter, not just a popular device for acting undemocratically and getting what you want before you have explored the alternatives. You do not resort to it just because you feel strongly enough on the subject in dispute to be willing to go to gaol for it. It is vital to be both committed and brave. But it is even more important not to antagonise the very people that you wish to convert.

However, there is still an immediate place for non-violent methods of social action. Effectiveness does not depend solely on civil disobedience: there are the legal forms of non-cooperation. In addition there is the untold wealth of innovative legal non-violent action - for new peace-inducing words, for new forms of peace-inducing action, for new methods of quenching wrath.

Chapter 6

THE PROBLEMS OF NON-VIOLENCE

In the course of this book I have drawn attention to many of the more defensible roots of violence, i.e., those which aspire to the respectability of being rational at least in a self-interested way. But the deepest of all violence's roots lies in a fact of life which pacifists should not only admit but emphasise: that if one goes on descending the ladder of escalation one does eventually come to a level of violence at which it is both indispensable and efficacious. Violence is needed. Criminals cannot be controlled through good sense and kindness; they need to be captured and sometimes segregated. Children have to be restrained from rushing out on to the street, violently if the child is in a tantrum and non-violent methods are not having the desired effect. Aggressors do sometimes need to be turned back from our frontiers, even if our society is a non-violent one.

My claim is that the existence of an admitted need for an indispensable minimum of violence has been conjured into a devils' 'open sesame' to every evil that violence can bring. - Yes, there is a level at which violence sometimes works and is certainly necessary. But, as we all know in moments of reflection, it does not follow from the fact that mild violence is needed either that homicidal violence is needed or that it is ever justifiable. On the other hand, it does pose a vital question for the non-violent human: 'Granted, it is possible for non-violent humans to exist - they have existed in many times and places. But can a non-violent society exist? Is it possible to build a society which carries out the indispensable functions of violence in a non-homicidal way?'

This is like asking the question which conscientious objectors faced in World

War II: am I being parasitic? Am I shirking one of the indispensable nasty jobs of a viable community? This is a perennial question: and my first claim in answer to it is that a fairly full rebuttal has already been presented. But we are so slow to learn the lessons of non-violence that some repetition is beneficial - especially from a somewhat altered perspective.

In what follows, I shall assume the wrong-headedness of war but still ask myself whether there are not more restricted forms of conflict in which homicidal violence is sometimes necessary and justified. To deal with all the different situations in which this sort of claim is made is obviously impossible. I shall restrict myself to three representative kinds of situation. What I say about these can serve as a guide to those which I do not discuss.

1.   So far from thinking that the function of law enforcement sometimes forces us to use homicidal violence, I wish to claim in what follows that law enforcement would be much more easily carried out in a non-violent country than in any other. Dispensing with lethal violence would actually improve the work of the police. It is precisely in violent societies that the function of law enforcement tends to break down; and it is their very violence which is responsible for the breakdown. Really good police work is only possible in a society that has reached a fairly high degree of non-violence and in which crime is relatively uncommon.

The armed righteous always seem to think that the level of violence needed depends on the degree of violence commanded by anti-social forces. But, to a much greater extent, it rests on how the collective deals with the problems of enforcement, including resorts to war. The less we enforce, above an indispensable minimum, the less enforcing we have to do.

Non-violent countries slice off the higher levels of enforcement at which nations pit themselves against one another and many millions of humans are slaughtered. They maintain that the very idea of enforcement at these levels is a social absurdity; inducements have to take the place of enforcements.

But law and order within the nation does require enforcement; and enforcement necessitates a minimum of violence. Would a non-violent society be able to hold this minimum below the level of lethal violence?

In my view, a non-violent country would have a police system that was far more genuinely two-tier than any system that has yet existed. This is because the general-public tier, the tier on which we are all potential enforcers or offenders, would be far more active and complete than such tiers ever are at present even in the Scandinavian countries.

Witnesses would always witness, though they would make the usual mistakes about what they claimed to see. And people would be quick to lend a hand in emergencies, rushing to the help of victims, siding against bullies or aggressors. Why should all this be so? Am I forecasting the emergence of utopia? To some extent I am - for the reason that turning to non-violence would be reflected in vast social reforms in all directions: it would be an absolutely key development in human life. For example, in a non-violent society the reform of the violent minority would only be enforced at a fairly low level of violence; and the less severe one is with the violent, the stronger the appeal which one is addressing to the non-violent sides of their natures - and such sides exist in us all.

But this example is very general. Let me raise a quite different one that must be admitted to be an everyday and also a vital matter.

When our street-level security systems are in an advanced state of decay, as they appear to be in many parts of the U.S.A., they have invariably become almost one-tier, witnesses being unwilling to witness let alone willing to join with the professionals in quenching wrath.

The law enforcement functions of a non-violent country presuppose the most rigid gun control, a constant effort being made to hurry guns to their ordained places in our chambers of horrors, and to disarm the population. Blunt instruments cannot be rounded up or declared illegal. Kitchens must contain knives that can double as lethal weapons. But when guns are absolutely banned homicide is driven back from massacre to murder. Mayhem is always with us but its scale is reducible.

Of course, rigid gun control raises immense problems. Gun-lovers are legion and are always a thorn in the community's flesh. Guns can be smuggled and illegally manufactured, etc., etc. But seeing guns as utter social poison could work wonders; and no non-violent policies can be implemented by a society that lacked such a conviction.

But, from time to time, gun control is bound to fail. When the bad lad of the street gets his finger on the now rare trigger, what is to be done?

I have already admitted that law enforcement requires some degree of violence. Must I now make a more damaging admission? For how are we to control homicidal maniacs without ourselves becoming homicidal? Law enforcement is supposed to quench violence, to stop it dead in its over-escalating tracks. But how is this to be done without going up and up the ladder of violence if you have to? Are you not driven to be as vicious as the other fellow?

You do need to control - yes. It is undeniable. But you do not need to kill in order to exercise needed control: you only need to disarm and thereby to enforce a de-escalation of the struggle. For example, when you take a killer's gun you force him to abandon shooting in favour of swearing, an improvement of life-saving proportions. 'But that's daft! How d'you take his gun while he's alive and pointing it at you?' The answer is that you must do what is now often done to straying and potentially dangerous animals: you must anaesthetise him, rendering him unconscious. Some modern anaesthetics are virtually instantaneous. And still more effective weapons of this kind are quite conceivable. The same ingenuity which has led to escalation must now be used to further de-escalation. My claim, then, is that stun guns, which only bring temporary helplessness, are sufficient to deal with all levels of violence up to the limits of law enforcement.

Stun guns would provide a non-violent society with its greatest compromise with the necessary evil of violence. Their use would represent the most violence that the society was prepared to inflict. They would see their use as both a last resort and as a saddening social failure, and therefore as a means which should be used only when more fatal violence can be stopped in no other way. Provided that guns only stun and recovery from being disabled by them is complete and rapid, there does not seem any reason for objecting to further improvements in this brand of weaponry. For example, stun guns could be made increasingly safe, increasingly instantaneous in their effects, and increasingly suited to dealing with automatic military weapons.

But stun guns are the least acceptable face of a non-violent society, and one that it would do its utmost not to have to show. This would be ensured by the fact that its enforcement agencies would be primarily concerned to do away with the need for enforcement. Their officers would be selected mainly for their readiness to give non-violent guidance rather than for their skills in enforcement. The knight in shining armour is a highlight of the battlefield. But his merits are still more dazzling when he takes his armour off and goes to work at the kitchen sink. It should be much the same with the law enforcement officer of a non-violent society.

Law enforcement in a non-violent society would be in the hands of an elite who were both gifted and versed in the uses of both violence and non-violence, especially the latter, and who showed fine judgment on when and how to use each of them. They would be aware that at best enforcement is only a passing victory, and that the war against anti-social forces can only be won by reform and reconciliation, by some form of personal development; and hence, that laws have to be enforced as reconcilingly as possible.

I shall now return to what I said earlier about systems of collective security being the only ones at the interpersonal level of security.

Collective security depends on people being ready to intervene when they see signs of victimisation. A police force can do all a society's dirtiest work, e.g., disarm dangerous bandits and killers. But police officers cannot be everywhere, either as witnesses or as enforcers: they need the constant help of the citizenry. But they cannot expect to receive much help when intervening is liable to get one shot. The price of intervention has become too high. And the only thing that can bring it down is pacification, or the building of a more non-violent society.

This is one of the things that I am mainly relying on when I speak hopefully about the potential achievements of non-violent law enforcement. It would be able to enlist more public support because the price of such assistance would have tumbled. Guns would have been controlled to the point of virtual elimination. Brutality would still be possible and would sometimes occur. But the good citizen who is willing to take on a bully who has only his bare hands to hurt with, is not willing to take on a hit man. At best, good citizens are heroic, not suicidal. Poor gun control, of the kind that bedevils police work in America, escalates law enforcement methods and tends to cut off the lower tier of the collective security system.

North American enforcement officers often say that the run of folk are only wanted as witnesses. Their involvement in enforcement would be a menace. This makes good sense in a country as violent as the U.S.A. You do not want amateurs about when professionals are trading shots. But if the criminal were disarmed by gun control and police action, would not the enforcement officer feel quite differently? The helper would be unlikely to collect anything worse than severe bruises. Furthermore, when arrest involves nothing worse than a fist fight, the arresting officer is glad to have the aid of a few extra fists. In a non-violent country special agents would welcome public support of every kind.

But a non-violent country is not only specially suited to running a system of collective security: it is also specially suited to pay for one. This is because it has jettisoned the burden of armaments and is probably many billions in pocket. This vast sum can be used to do two vital things: pay for exceptionally high-level social services and security services.

Both reinforce public support. But in this context it is the security services which most deserve to be stressed. Nothing is a worthier cause in any society than that of raising the level of police recruitment. It is obvious that much has been done in this direction in recent times. Sound political judgment is now expected from senior officers. Intelligence is expected from detectives. Humanity is expected from the officer on patrol. And the fact that these expectations are fulfilled less often than we should like does not lessen the fact that such expectations have replaced those of bovinity and unthinking brutality. But clearly, much more is needed.

A non-violent society would also spend very large sums on surveillance. Some of the kinds needed elsewhere would have become superfluous. But they would need to be replaced by vigilant gun control officers who checked smuggling and searched out secret caches of weapons.

A non-violent society would not be one which hoped to skimp financially on its security: it would simply be one that demanded more for its money.

2.   There are times when we do not only want to defend (or to protect) people, we want to make them safer than we are ourselves: we want to create what I have called security differentials. Violence can certainly create these, even though it is uniquely threatening to all. I have referred repeatedly to Bush's visit to Colombia - safe in a security nightmare, his power towering above the inferno. Well, what about a non-violent country? Can it create the security differentials which it may need or want? The answer is that it can

and cannot.

Within its own heartlands, where weapons are rigidly controlled and an effective two-tier system of collective security is in operation, there is clearly no problem. Non-violent security methods can do relatively little to make one person safer than another - though they can certainly do more than they seem able to do when you first think about it, e.g., by concealing people or with the help of stun guns. but they do not need to offer much special protection: ordinary levels of security are high enough for anyone. We have entered a different world - a world of high security and low differentials.

But what about the risks at the many points where a non-violent country borders on countries that do not have a commitment to non-violence and are on bad terms with it? The leaders of a non-violent country do not need, like Bush, to go unscathed into the lion's den: they do not need to retain a top place in the world by underlining their own might. But there are many circumstances in which it would be very difficult to prevent leaders from being at serious risk. Four American presidents have been assassinated. That is an appreciable percentage of the total and makes the office one of the most dangerous that anyone can occupy. But it might be claimed that its riskiness fades before that of being a non-violent leader of a country that is under attack.

Gandhi and Martin Luther King Jr., were both assassinated: the risks of occupying such positions as theirs are certainly great. Nevertheless, they are liable to be exaggerated. For two reasons. First, moral and spiritual greatness is protective. Take the Gandhi case. The sight of a man who combines physical frailty with fearless gallantry is deeply stirring; and the will to injure tends to be stayed in such circumstances. He was killed eventually, of course. But only after he had liberated India with powers that did not grow out of the barrel of a gun. Even in King's case the assassination could have been much more damaging socially than it was. King's work was by no means done. But he had chosen and prepared the way for his successors; and that is sometimes, though not always, a blessing. More important, non-violence had taken root in one segment of the Afro-American liberation movement, disciplining and restraining it. For non-violence has not only been a direct blessing, bringing about its own characteristic effects; it has also been a blessing indirectly, through what it has done to turn what might have been unrestrained violence, into almost token violence. As in some American cases, it is Mandela's restraint that has been impressive, not the violence of his followers. He might as well have been non-violent for all the good that his violence has done him - and he has lost all the advantages that outright non-violence would have brought him.

Furthermore, as I have already stressed, a non-violent community is not entirely weaponless. It still has its stun guns and there is no reason why these should not be models of their kind: minimising the risks of permanent or lethal injury, and maximising its disabling effects on its victims. We are apt to forget that a stun gun can be as good at stunning as a homicidal gun is good at killing; and a stunned man is as good as dead for the time in which he remains stunned.

Nonetheless, casualties among non-violent leaderships are highly probable; and they could be immensely damaging to the movements concerned. They could also be a discouragement to the second rank of their leadership. Gandhi himself was always ready for death. But how could his liberation movement have spared him? He was the Mahatma, a mortal god, and the continued existence and dedication of his non-violent movement depended on his being there to guide and inspire it. Suppose that Gandhi had been assassinated at the time of the Round Table Conference in the 'thirties. I am sure that the Indians would have returned to the struggle. But would the independence cause have remained non-violent? and If not, would it have succeeded? Or succeeded so quickly?

This is not a healthy state for any movement: to have a leader who - at least in the short run - is probably indispensable. Having a great leader is a supreme blessing, of course. Greater health does not lie in becoming less responsive to exceptional quality in your leaders. It is part of the common man's coming of age to welcome the aristocrat. But as Gandhi showed when he discouraged the use of the term 'Mahatma' in relation to himself, a mortal god is a contradiction, and that what is wanted is not a mortal god but a 'bapu', a true father of the people, who can say what it wants before it has clearly discovered it for itself. Besides, in the fullness of time we outlive 'bapu', however unwillingly. Fathers are essentially dispensable.

The first thing that can be done to lessen the indispensability of leaders can be, and usually is, done by the leaders themselves. They perform this service when they become teachers as well as leaders. Gandhi is the obvious case in point. He was every bit as great a teacher as he was a leader. He was a journalist on a massive scale; and much of his journalism consists of teaching rather than here-and-now leading. The result is that Gandhi still leads, much as a good father continues to offer an example and may continue to convey a message long after his death. Thanks to scholars and others we now know a great deal about his methods and campaigns; he gives us posthumous guidance. And so, when Gandhi was assassinated, although his flair and insight were lost, his teaching and example survived.

The remainder of the problem is less a matter of leadership than of followership. A good followership not only chooses better leaders, it is also better able to cope if anything happens to them. A good followership does still consist of followers, admittedly. But though even good followers still need leaders to tell them what to do next, they can tell themselves what NOT to do next - and this is usually enough to keep them going till more natural leaders emerge. And so we have to set out to build a good followership as part of our answer to our leadership problem. A good followership needs outstanding leaders, as all followers do. But when it has been temporarily robbed of its outstanding leaders it can take care of itself till they have been replaced.

What is a good follower in this context? Someone who is a fitting user of the moral weapon. He and she live in a state of moral alertness - aware of their moral agency, aware of their responsibilities, aware of partings of the ways, ever open to reason, and always humane. This is a considerable achievement, as we all know. Relatively few attain it. But there seems to be no invincible reason for not attaining it. And there can be no doubt that it is the main part of the answer to mortality in high places.

What can we do to become better followers? We can become more recollected about our moral agency - more constantly aware that we can act well or badly, and that it can make all the difference which we do.

We can also vastly improve our educational systems. At present - as I know through long contact with university students - we can reach both mature years and a university without ever having heard of morality - except perhaps as something people believed in before they started to live together without being married. High tech. and 20th century doubts have hurried it out of the curriculum. 'All one really needs to remember is that one lives in a free country' - and that means that although there are some things one should not do, no one is entitled to object if one DOES decide to do them. For criticism - any criticism - is intolerable.

What needs to be taught can be simply approached through any newspaper. It is our eye on the world; and is as good at opening the moral eye as anything we might use. Riots and other ill-considered bursts of violence can be considered. Likewise passing acts of terrorism - gone, forgotten, unavailing. Except, of course, that the dead stay dead. Unemployment, poverty, social differences, sexual differences. Any newspaper is a superb educational document, if it is read with any attention and understanding.

Finally, the practice of non-violence is itself a forcing house of better followers. You know that what you are makes all the difference to its effectiveness; and what you are relates mainly to your stewardship of your moral agency, and what you might do to improve that stewardship. This is indeed one of the main reasons for the practice of non-violence. It concentrates the thoughts of those who practise it on their conduct, not narrowly and fanatically, but reasonably and responsibly. Again, the use of non-violent methods requires great courage, persistence and discipline. If you try to use non-violent methods without possessing these qualities, your emphatic need for them is going to encourage your further development.

Summing up, then, it can be said - yes, the vulnerability of leaders can be a problem for a non-violent community or movement. But it is never just a problem: it is also a challenge.

3.   Let us suppose that in some way or other all the large obstacles to its happening are surmounted and a marauding band with political ambitions starts to operate within a non-violent country.

'It's a walkover' says their leader. 'These folks are wide open. We'll topple their government in seconds flat. Those old-time conquistadors will have nothing on us'.

My claim is that this leader (whom I shall call 'Rambo') is mistaken, and that his conquistador-type attack will be like shooting bullets into bales of cotton. Although the bullets are armour-piercing and the cotton is soft, their momentum will be spent before they reach the end of the bales of cotton. Similarly, long before Rambo is in a position to take over the presidency and give his first order, his attack would have been quenched and he would be admitting that he could not make any real progress.

The cotton starts to slow him as soon as he crosses the frontier. He is a marauder and not attempting to hide it. All those who live in the vicinity of the intruding gang would have been put on the alert. 'Homicidal intruders. No cooperation or obedience. Disarm, if opportunity afforded'. They would be given no food, no shelter, nothing - unless, of course, they allowed themselves to be disarmed. In addition, a Special Security Squad, the cream of the enforcement crop, would be homing on to Rambo's party with their stun guns and their sane counsels.

But let us suppose that his luck continues to hold and that he begins to kill his way towards what he believes is the capital. He is not finding it easy. The Special Squad is dogging his steps and he is having to concede that these peaceniks do not seem to know that power grows out of the barrels of his guns. He has had to spill a lot of blood and he does not seem to be getting anywhere.

Cotton would also be supplied by the local political institutions which would have several unusual features. First, they would involve the minimum of centralisation, making it relatively hard to distinguish the country's head from its tail. Second, office-bearers would have been trained both in rapid transfers of power and in going underground. The baton of government would be passed or hidden as soon as it seemed likely that its possession would be contested. And so poor Rambo, slowed on every side by non-cooperation, would not even know whom to kill next. He would also have to count his bullets in this strange disarmed society.

'Can you call them civilised?' he exclaims. 'They've nothing worth a damn to kill with . . . . I want to go home'.

4.   Terrorism is probably thought of as a problem for believers in Gandhian non-violence since it seduces revolutionary leaders who might otherwise be attracted by the moral weapons of civil disobedience and non-cooperation. This lamentable seduction does occur. In spite of its repeated failures and the successes that can be attributed to the use of non-violence, there are still many people who, frustrated in any course for which they would claim social value, at once incline to the use of terrorism. It is almost as if the willingness to kill is seen as a watershed in the development of convictions: you have reached maturity if they drive you to killing other humans.

To this it might be replied, 'But it is kill or be killed with the terrorist. He only takes life at serious risk to his own'. This is often not true: the serious risks are only taken by the terrorist's victims. For the victims of murderous attacks their deaths are a certainty - and these victims did not know that they had been targeted or were running risks. The dangers they run, unlike those of terrorists, are not dangers which they voluntarily accepted, They do not accept the risks as the price of serving a cause: they are just compulsory victims of it - condemned to die in causes other than their own.

Yes, terrorism - qua method of social action - is clearly an alternative to the non-violence of the strong. But from a moral point of view they are no more in competition than the sun and a pit of darkness. The non-violent insist on the indivisibility of justice, and do not wrong any in the pursuit of the limited objectives which they themselves seek: the terrorist does not even consider justice for all, the only justice he seeks is justice for himself. And further, because he sees his own cause as just, he believes himself entitled to victimise others in pursuit of his goal. Terrorism appeals to the fear that has a large place in most of us.

As a more popular alternative to non-violence, terrorism certainly deserves a place in our discussions. But it also deserves a place in them because it is the very antithesis of the moral weapon. After all, one is the non-violence of the strong and just, and the other is the violence of the weak and unjust - those who are weak enough to resort to any means whatsoever to gain their ends. One represents the peak of moral discrimination: the other represents the pit of moral indiscrimination. It is therefore deserving of special and unique castigation.

But what is terrorism? The question is worth asking for at least two reasons:

first, because present-day terrorism is quite a different thing from the terrorism of the past; and second, because it trades morally on a relatively forgivable past.

Today terrorism is organised intimidation and depends on fear in much the same way as protection racketeers. Terrorists live by making threats and then carrying them out ad nauseam, their hope being that they will induce such fear in the populace that it will pressure the relevant government into altering a situation or policy in some desired way. They are fear and death merchants and represent a large decline from the moral level of arms' dealers.

But, in its beginnings, terrorism was assassination, something that is far more discriminating and defensible. Again and again, human political ineptitude has thrown up the social cancers that we call tyrants - Hitlers, under one name or another. But I myself prefer preventative to curative methods: I would rather stop the development of this political malignity than resort to the knife or the bullet. But it is hard not to see some assassins as liberators as well as terrorists.

The changes are due to many things: modern methods of defending tyrants; contemporary methods of communication and publicity-mongering; the development of institutions and ideologies which go at least some way towards proofing societies against the sometimes vast disorders generated by assassination; and the decline in the absoluteness and lawlessness of rule and rulers. Julius Caesar was not only a dictator with absolute power, he had a personal style of government which came to be feared and even hated: killing Caesar ensured great changes and just MIGHT preserve Rome's republican character. The assassins did alter the course of events very fundamentally - but in directions opposite to those desired. They brought about their own political defeat and the victory of the very things which they were striving to prevent. But it might have gone differently . . . . They had some chance of success: most terrorists today have absolutely none. They kill and kill, never seeming to weigh in the balances the political cost-ineffectiveness of their methods. What they do is growing worse and worse - escalating as weapons escalate - and their excuses for doing it are getting less and less plausible.

Today, in the more developed parts of the world, democracy (in some degree or other) prevails. Kennedy was reachable, and a personal style of presidential rule was eliminated. But the American constitution ensured that he would be succeeded by a certain previously-chosen individual and that this individual would follow many of the same policies as Kennedy had been following. Also, presidents would have kept popping up in an orderly way no matter how many assassins killed - and they are lucky to be able to kill any, as the case of Bush in Colombia makes clear. Security differentials can now defeat all but the very luckiest of assassins. And the assassinations, if they occur, make less difference than they used to make. It has become easier to pick on the ordinary Joes of this world, partly because they are easier to influence and partly because democracy has placed the fate of governments in their hands. And so the new plan is to make ordinary Joes and Jills so afraid for the skins they love, including their own, as to alter their policies in such a way as to meet terrorist demands.

The I.R.A. is a case in point. It is always managing to kill people, especially the wrong ones; but what has it contributed to its cause? Well, clearly it has contributed far less than nothing - so much less, in fact, that its cause would probably have triumphed by now if the I.R.A. had never existed. In brief, it is likely that it has actually delayed the long-term inevitability of Irish unity.

A further word on escalation in relation to terrorism. As weapons escalate, the murderousness of terrorism escalates. Once upon a time, terrorists used blunderbusses: now they use automatic pistols and bombs: tomorrow - and who can say how soon? they will use nuclear, chemical and bacteriological methods. Terrorism has to be reduced to old-style assassination. And rigid gun control is the only way in which this highly desirable end can be achieved.

It is on grounds such as those I have been discussing that I claim that while terrorism has been getting ever more murderous, it has also been getting steadily less effective.

Chapter 7

CONFLICT AND INTERVENTION

All that I still wish to do is to stress two things that are vitally connected with non-violence: the potential creativeness of social conflict and disagreement; and the need to intervene early against undesirable developments.

1.   One of the great achievements of human life is the capacity to make conflict minister to the needs of all humans, both weak and strong.

Among other animals conflict simply weeds out the weak; and so, at best, it is mainly of benefit to the species, not individuals, even the strong. Among humans conflict has always been a vastly more complex phenomenon, apt to stir ingenuity and thereby to be of benefit to all, but still more likely to result in clashes of kinds that have become so damaging that they threaten the survival of the species. The creativeness of conflict was always present. But its destructiveness bids fair to be of permanently greater importance. This is due to immediate furies and follies, and to the refusal to give close attention to the conditions that have to be met before conflict can be creative.

That conflict and disagreement can be creative is now widely recognised. For example, at many small gatherings of business executives and perhaps politicians, differences of opinion are often used to stimulate new ideas, and thereby to turn superficial conflict into higher forms of cooperation. This is only possible if there is fundamental accord of the sorts which should exist between executives of the same company or between ministers of the same government. It is also essential that there should be considerable flexibility of mind - or the bounciness that enables individuals to give and take, to collide without feeling hurt or diminished. Rubber balls bounce: cannon balls only clash or split. If we are unbending, on distant or merely formal terms, we are unlikely to have fruitful exchanges. We are then more likely to bruise than to bounce, and are happiest when we do not quite touch.

This does not mean that creative exchanges are ruled out by reserve, introversion, sensitiveness, etc.: it simply means that they have to be differently engineered. Nearly all of us have known intimate relations with some human beings. Nearly all of us know what it is like to see deeper or to enjoy other benefits as a result of having had clashes with others. What we need to do is to train ourselves to be catalysts of our own styles of creative relations with those with whom we disagree, bringing out the bounce in ourselves by discovering underlying accords and by recognising others' merits.

It can also be useful to engineer some kinds of conflict within ourselves, e.g., by making the best cases we can for points of view to which we are opposed, by setting ourselves to achieve deeper understanding of alien outlooks and even personalities.

When dogs play they bite, sometimes running in circles and even biting their own tails. But nobody is hurt because nobody is trying to hurt. They are going through the motions of fighting without actually fighting, like actors on a stage; and this sort of make-believe seems to be the greatest fun in a dog's life. It is the discovery of play and probably the most creative thing that dogs ever do. It is much the same in human life. We bounce best when we are playing - when we enjoy the bouncing and engage in it for its own sake as well as for its results. We need to be serious and committed, certainly. But we should retain the bounciness of play, avoiding solemnness or loss of sense of proportion. We need to distinguish play from the main concerns of life, of course. But with the exception of worship, which is the concern of religious people only, a certain playfulness should always be retained; and unless we retain it the creativeness of conflict is very hard to maintain.

Unfortunately, play-fighting dogs often arouse one another's anger and what started as fun degenerates into earnest strife and fake bites change to hard nips. Here, too, it is much the same in human life. Escalation can start anywhere and end anywhere, one thing leading to another till all the combatants are dead. This may yet be the story of human conflict. But that need not be the case if we take the first great step towards making conflict creative: proofing it against destructive escalations. The necessary beginning of all such proofing is to swear off killing - to vow that, as far as we are concerned, killing is to be taken out of conflict entirely and unconditionally.

When we all know that serious disputes will not escalate into homicidal madness we are freer to speak up and also to hear the unvarnished truth from others. We have set out on a path that might make all conflict creative.

But non-violence of one sort or another is not only the beginning of creative conflict, properly understood it is also the end of it. For, as we use the moral weapon more and more effectively we become better and better at putting conflict at the service of cooperation. Indeed, these activities are essentially one: the non-violent arts are the arts of creative conflict.

'Yes, perhaps. But you speak as if the humane and rational were always on the same side of the fence. And they aren't. Some conflicts force us to take sides, and we find humane and rational people on both sides'.

Over a period of time this often ceases to be true - and therefore, we should bear in mind the possibilities of future accord. The slavery issue is a case in point. When some Quakers first opposed it in the 17th century it was accepted by multitudes of relatively good men and women. But gradually, over a considerable tract of time, they all came to see that it made poor economic sense as well as moral anathema. This is how it has often been. The humane and rational are divided at first. But as they learn to see deeper than immediate self-interest that which has hitherto been widely or universally accepted becomes intolerable and there is virtual consensus on the issue.

'But sometimes basic human divides come into view and no resolution of the conflict is possible. This is surely the case with the present struggle between pro- and anti-abortionists?'

To some extent I think this is true. As far as any of us can see at present, the divide between the religious and the non-religious is unbridgeable. Nothing creative seems likely to emerge from that head-on confrontation. But does it make sense to be sure of this? When the narrowness and prejudice and dogmatism virtually disappear from the religious scene (as seems likely in a century or two) many of the irreligious may think less one-sidedly about religious questions.

However, even if we disregard such possible developments, the statement I am considering is more false than true. This is because such divides can teach us much about how ultimate disagreements should be dealt with.

The abortion disagreement may not be resolved over a period of time, as were the slavery and racist issues. But in spite of the possible irresolubility of the dispute it has led to little blood-letting, mainly because humane and rational people have usually been in charge of both camps. Both sides have been pro-life about organisms whom they recognised to be people, only disagreeing to a relatively minor extent about how the term 'person' should be used. And the best of people on both sides have had close friends in the opposing camp. As a result, being a profound opponent has been altogether divorced from being an enemy. Both sides are slowly learning how to agree to differ. They are taking the necessary steps towards sharing a peaceful world.

All conflicts cannot be equally creative. Some can lead us on to views and practices that are superior to those previously accepted and followed: others can only teach us how to take the Cain out of human brotherhood.

2.   As far as can be seen at present, conflict is only creative in smallish doses that can physic the system. In the main, conflict has to be prevented. How is this to be done? Mainly through early forestalling intervention. For example, conflict is most easily controlled when it can be foreseen but has not yet arisen. People who refuse to be stopped might once have been advised. People who have to be forced might once have taken a hint. People who will not listen might once have been encouraged to act differently. Early intervention is the supreme trick of social well-being - but few seem to believe that it can be learnt and still fewer have the least intention of learning it. And so we do little to devise an earlier intervention society that might save many lives and much treasure.

The non-violent believe in early intervention because the earlier the intervention the more non-violent it is likely to be. They also believe that one can set oneself to become a good early intervener.

I once attended a performance of a Rabindranath Tagore play in a London church hall. As I waited with others in the gallery of the hall for the play to begin, a small company of youths arrived - on trouble bent. I groaned inwardly, foreseeing disturbances and interruptions. But, knowing my own limitations, I stayed in my seat. Fortunately, the wife of a well-known advocate of non-violence was also present; and as soon as the youths showed an inclination to annoy others she went over to them, and after a talk of several minutes persuaded them to be accommodating. Her intervention was wholly successful. No one lost a word of the play because of those youths; and the youths, for all I know, may have benefitted permanently from the brief talk and also from listening to the play. But I think it needs to be stressed that such interventions are best made, not by those who have screwed up their courage to the sticking point, but by those who have the maturity and good-will needed to make them successfully.

We have all heard forestalling quietening words: we have seen wrath being quenched. And we all know that success largely depends on early intervention as well as on personal development. For example, in the case I have just described, the intervention may well have been unavailing if it had been left till later, after the youths had moved into a more active phase, and a higher degree of confrontation had become inevitable.

Unfortunately, we have built a late intervention world.

Take the legal-illegal distinction, our main instrument for deflecting human conduct from the anti-social to the social. We all know that in many parts of the modern world this distinction is not enabling the community to uphold the good life. Crime has become Big Business; and something which is supposed not to pay has become the shortest cut to a billion dollars. Witnesses refuse to witness: instead, they are killed or corrupted. And when hoodlums are not taking someone for a sucker they are taking him for a ride. You can buy and sell the parts of many of the security agencies with which you come into contact. And if the law refuses to look the other way you can hire the best lawyers, some of whom can even reinterpret the law, forcing the legal-illegal distinction into shapes that neither legislators nor the public ever wanted. You can start law suits that bleed away the financial substances of your opponents. You can use your wealth to conjure perjured witnesses from the thinnest air. You can even buy legislators to do your business in high places. In a word, you can use your money to turn all the resources of law against themselves.

As I have been pointing out, this can be done in many ways. But underlying all these ways is one central condition of criminal success: that the criminal is innocent till proved guilty. This rule ensures that intervention will at least be late and that it will often not occur. It also ensures that it will usually be unavailing.

'Don't tell me you'd actually displace the presumption of innocence, one of the greatest bulwarks of freedom? Why, it is the basis of any half-decent society'.

This claim is often made in ignorance, its markers being apparently unaware that there are highly civilised countries of which it is false. Nevertheless, it is true that there have been many occasions in the past when the need to prove your guilt is all that has stood between you, and even your children, and being transported or hanged. But is this traditional rule still the best that can be devised? Or should it perhaps give place to a more flexible rule? For example, why should we all be tried under the some rule, regardless of whether we have been good citizens or our guilt - like Al Capone's - has become notorious throughout the country and even the world? What rule would Illinois have elected to have him tried under if it had been consulted? - asked secretly and on a scale that made vote-buying impossible? When guilt has become a household word it is farcical to presume innocence and you should be required to establish it. Capone was put away in the end. But he would have been put away much sooner, less bloodily, and to the greater public good, if he had been brought to trial under the guilty-till-proved-innocent rubric. When guilt has become a public joke it is time for the man in the street to show that he is no longer amused.

We have created a society in which small-scale crime is apt not to pay, but in which large-scale crime is supremely paying. The truth is that the peaks of crime can no longer be climbed by the authorities. Instead, those peaks need to be detonated, blasted to smithereens. What we need is a Night of the Short Shrift at the end of which the world's entire mafias and their followers would have been plucked - and permanently plucked - from the population.

But this is only the grossest instance of the need for earlier intervention. Thoroughly rotten apples need to be removed from the barrel, regardless of the legal niceties that unscrupulous brains have engineered for their protection. But it also has to be remembered that if society had intervened still earlier those apples may have been only bruised or even undamaged. Society's short arm of love has to outgrow the large arm of the law. Whoever you are, and however bad you are, you were probably once reachable; and it is our job, as your neighbours not only to keep you reachable but actually to reach you before the currents of delinquency sweep you away. Of course it is difficult to do this! But it is not made easier by failing to stress early intervention.

To some extent our failure in such matters is very like the main failure in our street collective security systems: they are not sufficiently two-tier. The public will cannot be represented by the police single-handedly, however well they are representing that will. They need our help - and when I say 'our' I am using the word with complete inclusiveness. The public will has to be represented by the Good Samaritan, not just by the sheriff.

Even the institutional devices of public concern, e.g., the social services, make heavy weather of early intervention. Again and again, in all modern societies, they are castigated for their failures to take action, for their refusal to abort tragedy by acting before it occurs - and as soon as it can be foreseen. But if the professionals are slow in intervening what sort of pace is to be expected from the man in the street? - the man who is only too apt to say that concerned action is not his business, and that just as he pays cops to chase robbers he pays social workers to prevent cruelty to wives and children.

Two-tiering our sustaining social institutions is immensely difficult. But they have to be two-tiered to function well. For just as the policeman is not always there when he or she is needed, the social worker is even less likely to be there when wives, children, old people and animals are being abused. We need to steer a much more active course between idle busy-bodying and neglect of social duty.

Small-scale early intervention has often been instituted, usually in forms that we are now disposed to ridicule, e.g., in ultra-polite society. For instance, in Jane Austen's *Pride and Prejudice* we are shown a society in which intervention is so early that its strongest sanction is social rebuff. This is illustrated by what Elizabeth said to Darcy when he first proposed to her and she accused him of 'ungentlemanlike' conduct. Needless to say, it took him months to accept such an appalling charge. But in the end he accepted it so humbly that his accuser was soon claiming (with her usual charm) to having been as great a social delinquent as he has been.

But our present informal and relatively democratic society of aggressive 'more-equals' is an unpromising one, if Jane Austen's world is any guide to the good life. The last thing we want is greater ceremony or any considerable show of politeness. But it is strongly arguable that greater formality would be beneficial if it could be combined with social democracy; and my belief is not only that it can but that in disguised forms this renewal of formality is already taking place in favoured corners of the world. The most obvious of these are connected with the planet-wide triumph of soap and water, of greater and greater cleanliness.

It is useful to remind ourselves of English's vocabulary of escalating intervention. The skeleton of such a vocabulary might run: 'to take an interest in', 'to encourage', 'to hint', 'to suggest', 'to advise', 'to insist', 'to enforce'. This is useful because it reminds us how varied intervention is, and of how comprehensively each of us is related to this scale. Some people are always encouraging: others are always hinting; some are always threatening and enforcing. Some of these interventions are thought of as manifesting hostility or superiority: others are not. Some are welcomed by those with whom your interventions bring you into contact: others are resented, some deeply. Some enlarge the scope of others' freedom: others narrow it. Some liberate and others imprison.

These forms of intervention not only differ hugely with respect to the responses to be expected from those with whose behaviour one has intervened: they also differ hugely with respect to people's willingness to engage in them. The result is that our short vocabulary not only charts a crescendo of intervention but also - in a rougher, less clear way - a crescendo of reluctance to intervene. For example, unless people are doing something clearly illicit or essentially private they are usually pleased to have others take some interest in them and to give them encouragement. And so there is seldom any reason to hesitate or to delay when one is disposed to be encouraging. It is hardly ever resented. Hinting, suggesting, guiding, are often resented. But the hint or advice is not infrequently taken even if some resentment is aroused. Certainly, a suggestion in season will be far less resented than insistence or chastisement at a later date, if one succumbs to the temptation of putting off counsel and eventually something has to be done. Also, if you feel bound to intervene forcibly later you will do so in desperation, with the greatest unwillingness, because you feel absolutely driven to it. You then realise that it would have been so much better to have faced the slight embarrassment that you might have felt if you had intervened earlier and proffered some sound advice.

Early intervention is easier, difficult as we often find it. If we delay, the likelihood is that some far more drastic kind of intervention will be imperatively needed.

We all suggest, advise and guide, whether we recognise it or not; and many of us do all these things badly, guiding others in ways that set them dreaming of escape from tutelage, not of how most to gain from our assistance. Many of these failures are remediable. We could take more care to discover the needs and preferences of the people concerned. We could take more pains over being tactful. We could become more aware of our own motives. And each of these advances would increase our effectiveness. 'Instruction' is a word that is not much liked nowadays. But the reality is that instructors come in all sizes and shapes. Some are adored and others abhorred.

Enforcement and punishment are escalations that are very liable indeed to be resented, often lastingly. But occasionally, if enforcement is seen as in the interest of those subjected to it, and therefore as a manifestation of good-will and even of friendship, it is not resented. And still more occasionally, punishment is felt as deserved and has reclaiming effects. But much more often, partly as a result of remediable things that have not been remedied, it gives rise to enmity and hatred.

A non-violent society would have a penal side to its institutions. But this penal side would not be concerned to impose pain and suffering - for that way enmity and unreachability lie; they would be simply designed to prevent crime and to reclaim criminals. This is the only way in which intervention, which is initially resented and seen as a sign of hostility, can mature into acceptance of proffered amity.

The model in all human relations is the loving family, the family in which space for growth is given and yet in which intervention is easy when some member starts to behave in a way that seems likely to cause trouble. In such a family, love is taken for granted. The motives can be relied upon; they are nearly always fundamentally good. And so, when a family member tries to amend your conduct, even their mildest interventions are often enough to set you questioning your behaviour. The young in such families usually want to be guided, and generally, inducted, into society. In fact, they often place very high value on it, and are appalled at the very idea of losing it. And the seniors allow for social changes, are aware of the differing needs of different people, and often show that they are aware of the particular needs of each family member. But all that I have said has to be interpreted sensibly with due allowances made for petty friction and the resulting squabbles. It is common, perhaps customary, to wax cynical and ribald, when such matters are raised. We are so determined not to be boastful in what we say about them; and hence, they bring out our humility as much as anything does.

Once, on holiday, my family boarded with another family. The relations between the members of that family were a revelation to me. My father and I were on respectful and basically loving terms: at a certain distance we got on well enough to pass muster in affectionate family circles. But this father was resplendent with fatherliness. So much so that it was a pleasure for me, as a son, to take note of his dealings with HIS son. He was a master of liberating interventions.

At present few things are more detested than any form of complaint or criticism. People who are normally quite reasonable are often inflamed by it. It matters little how justified any reasonable person would think it - if he were only willing to listen. The criticism is taken badly on principle - as being criticism. To be complained about is an affront. For example, daily on our roads one can see drivers committing actions that are both dangerous to others and illegal, and then reacting with fury when one of their victims dares to object. No self-criticism, fairness or understanding is shown, no willingness to engage in a short spell of open-minded listening. My human rights are coming to be seen as including, if not a right to be thought perfect, at least a right to be thought every bit as perfect as anyone else - and therefore as immune from criticism.

But this is not only plain folly but a desperate threat to the possibility of early intervention. We are all prone to error, and as the world's complexity increases human fallibility is more abundantly illustrated. We all need guidance. And one of the best measures of good sense is the way one takes criticism. For what can do more for quick learning than having an open ear and a good grace when one is being guided?

And this draws our attention to something that we can all do for early intervention: we can make well-intentioned intervening easier. We should mind our own business - yes. But civilisation also depends on our being ready to mind other people's business too, in appropriate circumstances - and such circumstances arise far more often than is recognised in any Western society.

Properly seen, non-violence is not only concerned to quench the wrath of war but to quench all wrath. It is a pervasive quenching, a continuing obligation to prevent conflict when it would be harmful, and to make the most creative use of it whenever it occurs. This is, of course, a counsel of perfection. But our present achievements fall far short of those which are attainable - especially with the help of early intervention. They also fall well short of the expectations that would be aroused in any intelligent alien species by the news that Man's name for himself is <u>homo sapiens</u>.